BIRTHING
THE WORD OF GOD

A LITTLE BOOK
ON CHRISTIAN PREACHING

By the Most Rev Dr Charles Jason Gordon
Archbishop of Port of Spain

Sophronismos Press
Louisville, Kentucky

First Printing: November 2020

ISBN: 978-1-7335457-4-7

ADDRESS:
27 Maraval Rd
Maraval
Trinidad and Tobago
Caribbean

Email: abcjg@catholictt.org

Cover photo by Elmo Griffith. Used with permission.

———————————————

**Other books by Archbishop Gordon may be found on
Amazon.com**

Encounters of Grace: A Pilgrim's Musing Along
The Camino de Santiago

Meditations in the Upper Room

Teach Us to Pray

CONTENTS

"Receive the Gospel of Christ whose herald you have become. Believe what you read, teach what you believe, and practice what you teach."

(Rite of Ordination)

Acknowledgements

I wish to thank the Rev John G. McDonald who has served as the Carl J. Peter Chair of Homiletics at the Pontifical North American College in Rome 2016-2019. Rev McDonald invited me to deliver the Carl J Peter Lecture in 2017. This pushed me to think more critically about preaching and to explore, in a systematic way, the art and science of preaching. He also read this work and offered invaluable suggestions to strengthen the final product.

Thanks also to Fr Guerric DeBona and Dr Rick Stern who invited me to deliver the annual Marten lecture of St Meinrad Seminary 2019. Their challenge and encouragement also led me to write on preaching and to rethink the fundamentals.

Msgr Cuthbert Alexander has been a constant support in proof reading my texts over the years. A big thanks for your care with this text. Thanks also to Felix Edinburough who did the final proofreading.

Fr Ronald Knott, thanks for the support through the Second Wind Guild that has made the publishing of this book possible. Last but not least, thanks to Tim Schoenbachler who did the technical work and graphic design to bring the manuscript to a book and publication.

So many people have given me feedback on preaching over the years. This has been invaluable in assisting me grow as a preacher. Thanks!

Most of all, glory be to God whose grace working in us can do infinitely more than we can ask or imagine (cf. Eph 3:20).

INTRODUCTION

This book is a compilation of my writings on preaching. It is intended to offer the reader a journey through the rudiments of preaching as a discipline, to the deeper calling of *mystagogue*. It is my belief that preaching is an under-utilised gift, that within the Church it is too seldom used to its full potential. A preacher who understands the rudiments and follows them with a sense of the depth of the journey, who furthermore has been initiated into the sacred mysteries, begins to allow the gift of preaching to mature in him and to offer fine aged wine.

From this perspective, preaching is a reflection of the depth and soul of the preacher. It is the dynamic ability to be intimate with God and to rely on the Holy Spirit to hear the word Christ is speaking to his Church in the present pastoral situation.

Preaching is an exact art. It is exact because it requires many practices that must be learnt and understood and done over and over and over. It is an art because the Word is born, "not of blood nor of the will of the flesh nor of the will of man, but of God" (Jn 1:13). It is in this drama, between practice of skills and falling into the hands of the living God that preaching is born.

By definition this requires vulnerability, relationship with God and the capacity to research and see the text in a different way – art and practice. The preparation is in your relationship with Scripture. How do you see Scripture? Just a text to read to find a sermon for Sunday? Or, is Scripture a place to go to encounter the living God? Here is the crux of the matter. If you want your preaching to move people to encounter Jesus Christ, then you need to have an active prayer life – to sit and wait and watch, regularly – to allow Christ to do in you what he wants.

Part of my preparation as a preacher has been an annual eight-day silent retreat which allows for a deep encounter with God. A life of grace is more precious than everything else. These are times when you fall into the hands of the living God and know that the unknown is more solid and secure than all else you can know. You live then in the midst of vulnerability and weakness and rely on God, knowing that God alone can see you through. This is not for the faint of heart. It is for those who are dissatisfied with the crumbs. We can become comfortable feeding our people with what is so unsatisfying.

God is birthing a new generation of priests for his Church. The question is whether you have the courage to stay the course, plumb the depth and journey with Christ through thick and thin. Our people know when we dish out cheap grace, cheap platitudes learnt from seminary and books we read. They know when we are fake and give just enough to impress, when the word comes from the head and when it comes from the heart. On every occasion they know, and they love us, and put up with us.

What if there was a generation of priests who chose to plumb the depths of the mystical way, the depths of humanity in all its frailty and vulnerability, and who chose to live in the unfinished state, waiting and watching and praying for God to finish the good work that was begun at baptism? What if there was a generation of priests who loved Sacred Scripture and pondered it day and night and savoured its sweetness and was nurtured in its incredible message of love?

What if there was a generation of priests who saw the sacraments as sacred mysteries or portals to the encounter with the Holy Trinity, a band of brothers willing to push past the apathy and suspicion about priests today, towards Christ himself the high priest who laid down his life for our sake and our salvation?

This book is for such priests, those who want to offer their congregations more than the routine, humdrum type of homily that neither feed nor unsettle. The time for mediocrity is long gone. Today's generation wants to encounter Christ each time they come to the liturgy. We owe it to them to prepare ourselves to give of our very best in the Sunday homily. Only then we can say: "We are unworthy servants; we have only done what was our duty" (Lk 17:10).

OVERVIEW

There is a logic to the book. The **first chapter** opens with a reflection on my relationship with Scripture. This, I believe, is fundamental to preaching. Look at your whole journey with Scripture, not just what you learnt in seminary. But, rather, how did you grow in understanding and knowledge of Sacred Scripture. Have you fallen in love with the Word who was made flesh? Has God ever spoken to you through the Scriptures? Ponder this for a while. How could you proclaim the incredible love of God if you have never experienced it or been blown away by it? You can speak about it, you can wax warm with many superlatives, but it will be like a man speaking about food who has never tasted it, never been nourished by it and never delighted in its smell and texture and unique pleasure with all the senses overwhelmed.

The **second chapter** is an exploration of the three main types of homilies. Through this investigation you are invited to delve into the main theme of the book "Birthing the Word of God". This is a big concept and one that requires significant spiritual discipline and incredible grace. The concept will be explored more fully later in chapter four. The purpose of this chapter is to tease the imagination and prepare the reader for the journey ahead.

The **third chapter** focuses on the purpose of the homily. We explore an ancient view of the homily, reflected in Nehemiah 8:8: The Levites expounded on the Law "making it clear and giving the meaning". Through this twofold process, the people were led to the encounter with God and came to repentance. They were renewed for the journey of rebuilding the wall and got the strength for all they needed to do. This chapter looks again at method in a focused way.

The **fourth chapter** reflects on the interconnection between the homily and the Eucharist. The journey of the two disciples to Emmaus is used as guide. The disciples only realised the encounter in the breaking of the bread. But looking back on the journey they realised their hearts were burning. This is the divine interconnection between Word and Eucharist. They both feed the disciple. The Word prepares for the encounter, and at the Eucharist the eyes are opened to see. This chapter is presenting another way of viewing the mystical dimension of preaching. It also demonstrates the integrity of the interconnection between Word and Eucharist.

The **fifth chapter** reflects on the sacred mysteries spoken about at the beginning of Mass. It wrestles with the inner demands of the Eucharist and thus the homily, which is supposed to point to the sacred mysteries. The reality is that so many people come to church and never experience an encounter with Jesus Christ. How is this possible if we are invited to participate in sacred mystery? The priest as mystagogue needs to initiate the people into the sacred mystery, for this he must first be initiated. The invitation here is to see the whole event of the Eucharist with a different lens – an initiation into this mystery.

The **sixth chapter** was written as a lecture for the annual Carl J Peter lecture, North American Collage in Rome. Here I lay out the methodology of preaching in a simple step-by-step approach. The big themes are preaching as a vocation, preaching with vision, *the dynamic of the text* and authentic Integral Human Development and preaching.

If you like, this is the 101-preaching guide, where I walk the preacher through the process I have used for preparation of the homily and demonstrate how this is integral to the spirituality of the priest. Either preaching flows from the priest's spirituality or it is merely oratory pointing to the giftedness of the priest and not to Christ who is the Word made flesh. In this chapter a theology of preaching is explored, and some practical steps given to achieve the goal.

The **seventh chapter** takes the reader through the agony and ecstasy of homily preparation. In this chapter you will see first-hand how I approach the text, the tools I use, the drama of preparation and the spiritual odyssey of moving through the darkness of not-knowing to insight, as the word is born. This is a practical step-by-step approach that gives you some check lists to ensure you go through the whole process of preparation, surrendering yourself to the living God.

The **eighth chapter** explores mystagogical preaching. German theologian Karl Rahner has said: "The Christian of the future will be a mystic or will not exist at all." These words haunt our Church today. People want the real stuff. For this, the priest needs to be willing to go to the depths of the tradition and initiate his people into the sacred mysteries.

To point the reader into this sacred mystery, Henri de Lubac's "The Motherhood of the Entire Church" is used as foundation. The Cardinal proposes the image of the birth and growth of the Word of God in the soul. Ultimately, this is about a Catholic imagination in the approach to Scripture and life.

The **ninth chapter** introduces the reader to one of the great ideas that undergirds the Catholic imagination in our time – authentic Integral Human Development. This concept which was first proposed by Paul VI and then reiterated by Benedict XVI is a touchstone for Catholicity today. We can all grow and develop and transcend our current limitations. By exploring this central notion, the preacher is faced with the challenge to become a continuous learner and striver for holiness. In addition, he is called to challenge the congregation to consistent growth and development in all areas of their lives.

The **tenth chapter** focuses on the stages of spiritual development which requires the utmost attention. It is imperative that the preacher understands the congregation's stage of development and his own. How do I do what is necessary to ensure continuous spiritual growth? How do I facilitate the congregation in the pilgrimage towards becoming fully mature in Christ?

It is the homily that is the best tool in the pastor's toolkit to aid the growth and development of his people. Fowler's stages of spiritual development and St Theresa of Avila's stages of prayer chart a path of development and offer an invitation to both preacher and congregation. The spiritual life, like all dimensions of human existence, is dynamic. We are capable of growth and development. The preacher needs to assist the congregation in understanding and desiring spiritual growth as an integral part of human maturation.

The **eleventh chapter** proposes feedback as a strategy for continuous improvement of the art and skill of preaching. By inviting feedback in a structured way, the preacher gets the tools to make incremental steps towards his improvement.

After all the theory and experiences communicated in this book, this is the one action step – if implemented and worked with continuously – that will improve your preaching dramatically over time. This is the one idea that I invite you to implement immediately. If you are part of a team preaching in the parish, a weekly meeting to discuss feedback will pay great dividends.

CHAPTER 1:

WANT TO ENCOUNTER CHRIST?
READ YOUR BIBLE

The Mass is an invitation to feed at three tables, the table of the Word, the table of the Eucharist and the table of service. Each of these is a portal into the mystery that is Christ. Each offers the disciple a way to encounter and become more deeply conscious of his or her union with Christ.

This portal, this offer of encounter, is not always seen or recognised, which does not mean it does not exist. It just means we need help finding entry into this sacred mystery.

Have you ever gone to the fridge to look for something which you knew was there? You opened the door, looked inside and did not see what you were looking for. Then someone came by and pointed it out and you realised it was there all the time. We do not need secret knowledge or esoteric thinking to find the portal. We do need to understand the Bible and the Eucharist for what they are – an opportunity to encounter Christ.

Catholics do not read the Bible?

There are many misconceptions about the Catholic Church and the Bible. The most frequent misconception is that Catholics do not read the Bible. The opposite is true. If you go to Mass every weekend, you will read all of St Paul and the four gospels every three years. If you go daily, you will read most of the Bible in two years. If you pray the Morning and Evening Prayer of the Church, you will read all the psalms every four weeks.

We understood bible-reading plans long ago. The Church broke the text into bite-sized passages and offered it to us as a way of reading the Bible continuously. The homily guided us to the deeper meaning of the passage and led us into an encounter. The Liturgy of the Word is intended to be an encounter with the living Word, requiring a mature relationship with the word.

A Magical Reading

In my early years, we had a picture Bible at home, and I remember flipping through its pages, fascinated by the pictures. The stories of Daniel and the lion, Moses and the basket, and the burning bush are all early memories. Our family also had a Bible given to my great grandfather in 1895. It was huge and occupied a place of prominence. It was always there.

As a teen, I acquired a Good News Bible, my first. It was easy reading and used modern terms. It spoke, for example, about the police arresting Jesus in the garden.

At Fatima College our RE teacher read Bible stories that were written in a dramatic way. It was captivating. I was part of youth and prayer groups that helped me to see the Bible as important.

My grandmother had read Bible stories when we were children. Now I began reading the Scripture in small doses. I began dipping into the Bible. The custom was to cut the

Bible, to pray for a word and just open the book randomly. Whatever your eye fell on was what God wanted for you. This was a hit or miss affair.

Sometimes, the words answered my quest with incredible precision; at other times they seemed to bear no relation. There was an assumption here. The Bible is God's Word and if you pray and believe, it will speak to you and shed light on your current situation.

A Sacred Portal

One weekend a group of us went on retreat at Mt St Benedict – four of us, young men on our own, for two days of prayer. By then, at 21, as a young adult, I had graduated to the Jerusalem Bible, with notes.

I prayed and opened the Bible as was the custom. My eyes fell on Isaiah 49. I felt like someone had ripped out my insides and turned me upside down! The Word came alive and hit me as it had never done before!

The words on the page became a living Word that has shaped the course of my life. This was the second time God proposed vocation to me. It had happened once before, at the end of Mass in the Fatima College chapel when I was 16. On that day, at the Mount, I understood the Bible was not a toy or a trinket to be played with for amusement. It was indeed the living Word of God that He used to speak to the heart of His people.

Then the Word of God became "...a lamp for my feet, a light on my path" (Psalm 119:105). No longer was it a matter of cutting the Bible, but devouring it, chewing portions in small bites at a time but relishing the Word and savouring its sweetness. I learnt that the words on the page were a portal that opens us to encounter with the Word who became flesh and lives among us. I learnt that Sacred Scripture was a way of prayer, and God speaks today if we have ears to hear and hearts disposed to listen. I learnt that Scripture is the Word of God.

Reading Scripture

From a living encounter with the Word of God as a young man, my scripture reading shifted to a study of the text in seminary. This evolved to the historical-critical method of exegesis in graduate school in Leuven, Belgium. This method of enquiry stimulated my intellectual curiosity. I could delve into a text, understand the layers, the textual variants, the words in the original language and the structure of the text, literary genre and, of course, the *Sitz im Leben* – the cultural, ethnic and social setting implied in the text and its world.

This academic study of the text opened the text and its many layers of interpretation. It was a demanding pursuit of knowledge that had its own rules. As a young priest my commentaries on the four gospels all held to the strict principles of historical criticism. Every week I would read the text of the week and then the commentary and all the notes on each word, each variant, each nuanced interpretation of the text. My gaze shifted from the Bible as an encounter with the Word of God to an encounter with intellectually stimulating ideas and connections that only few would find.

This subtle shift to a positivistic hermeneutic, was so imperceptible that I did not see it. The Bible now became the place to go to get a Sunday homily. The homily was about discovering in the text "things both new and old" (Mt 13:52). But all the time there was something else at work.

In Leuven I went for retreat to Namur, the formation house of the Jesuits. Father Michael, the formation director, introduced me to the Ignatian method of prayer: praying with the Bible. This brought harmony to my approach to the Scripture: my former way and now the historical-critical way. These two lived in me as separate islands of knowledge. I would use either approach but could not evaluate which was the most appropriate one to use. A faith perspective and a rationalistic positivistic perspective lived side by side. I chose, as is the advice of the parable of the wheat and the darnel, to leave them to grow till harvest time (Mt 13:24-29). For years I lived between these two perspectives moving unannounced from one to another.

In the year 2000, while doing my doctoral work in London, things changed. At the funeral of Cardinal Basil Hume, it was like a light was turned on and the world became three dimensional. Now I could see, but "people were looking like trees" (Mk 8:24). A 30-day retreat in 2004 and annual eight-day retreats began the process of integration and discernment. I would agonise over the text and mull over minute details until it yielded up its treasure.

George Lamming, celebrated Caribbean writer and intellectual, speaking about the process of interpretation had very uncharitable things to say about the historical-critical method:

The domain of mediation is restricted by the mediator's inhibiting sense of his role in expanding the terrain of mediation. This deformity at the critical level has had negative consequences for writers and those who diagnose what has been written. Diagnose is not an inappropriate word for men and women who insist on calling themselves doctors. ... The text is, indeed, spread out like a patient, and after the most meticulous dissection, it becomes etherised. There is a smell of bandages emanating from those accumulated footnotes, a certain odour of morphine lingers over the average thesis (16).

My positivistic hermeneutic was being challenged from the very discipline where the science emerged. The challenge came from a New World writer who understood the harm and shortfall of the Old World positivistic rationality.

The Ratzinger Challenge

I have to thank Joseph Ratzinger, theologian *par excellence* for jolting me out of a smug settled hermeneutic (way of interpreting the text). In Part Two of his book on *Jesus of Nazareth*, he said something that challenged my view of interpretation of the biblical text:

One thing is clear to me: in two hundred years of exegetical work, historical-critical exegesis has already yielded its essential fruit. If scholarly exegesis is not to exhaust itself in constantly new hypotheses, becoming theologically irrelevant, it must take a methodological step forward and see itself once again as a theological discipline, without abandoning its historical character. It must learn that the positivistic hermeneutic on which it has been based does not constitute the only valid and definitively evolved rational approach; rather, it constitutes a specific and historically conditioned form of rationality that is both open to correction and completion and in need of it. It must recognize that a properly developed faith-hermeneutic is appropriate to the text and can be combined with a historical hermeneutic, aware of its limits, so as to form a methodological whole (xiv, xv).

I was reading this book during Lent 2012, my first Lent as a bishop. I had a violent reaction to the text above. It seemed to me that the Holy Father, writing in his personal capacity as a theologian, was challenging the well-established historical-critical method of interpreting the Bible. He was proposing that we sneak faith into the interpretation *a priori*. This to me, violated the rules of interpretation. This text haunted me and upset me and rattled my cage. I found myself in long imaginary debates with the author.

One year later, at the annual meeting of the bishops of our region we learnt about ABP – Biblical Animation of all Pastoral life, which asks that we begin our pastoral planning with *lectio divina* to allow the Word of God to shed light on the pastoral problematic and so illumine the way forward for the Church. This was implemented in both Bridgetown and Kingstown where I was bishop. It was amazingly fruitful. The method introduced a new dynamic in our pastoral life – discernment. We stood before the pastoral and the biblical and asked how the word of God illumined the pastoral. The method was simple: we used the Sunday readings, regardless. It always spoke eloquently and with precision to the pastoral challenge at hand and gave us a new perspective.

Hermeneutic of Faith

Slowly my eyes were being opened to the perspective of Benedict XVI. I was beginning to see the Word of God alive, active and dynamic in the life of the Church. I was also beginning to see the problem with the historical critical method. I was now like the man in Mark's Gospel who began to see, but he saw people looking like trees (Mk 8:24). This stage continued as I tried to reconcile the preferred method of interpretation with what Ratzinger called a hermeneutic of faith.

George Lamming, speaking about hermeneutics says:

I would propose that the essential and supreme function of the critic/intellectual, in our circumstances, is to be a mediator of text; and the area of mediation must travel beyond the enclave of specialist and student, or specialist in contention with specialist. It must attempt to travel beyond this domain of mediation to link the human substance of the text to the collective consciousness, the continuing social reality which has, in fact nurtured the imagination of the writers (16).

The imagination of the biblical writers was nurtured by a unique faith perspective that was the pivotal axis around which the text and the plot was given shape. It was not that faith was being squeezed into the hermeneutic uncritically. It was rather that faith gave shape to the text and it was imbedded in the text as an essential dimension of the text. Writers like Scott Hann and Brant Petrie both use this hermeneutic of faith with great benefit.

Petrie asks the question, "What would a first century Jew have heard while reading this text"? By focusing on the original hearers of the text, faith is illumined as an essential dimension. The modern reader will not hear the text in the same way. By closing this gap between faith and the biblical text, the world of Scripture opened to deliver its treasures. My approach to preaching is indebted to this journey of recovering what I knew as a boy, but now with a fuller understanding of the way God works in and through the human interaction with the biblical text.

Space of Encounter

Recovering the Bible as an encounter with the Word of God is a great treasure. The texts of several Christian traditions indicate a great concern about the move away from reading the Bible as a source of the spiritual life. In the Catholic tradition two ecclesial texts, the Vatican II document, *Dogmatic Constitution on Divine Revelation - Dei verbum* (1965) and Benedict XVI's Post-Synodal Apostolic Exhortation - *Verbum Domini* (2008) have pointed to a way of receiving the Bible as an encounter with Christ, the Word who became flesh. They have also spelt out the dangers of the rationalist hermeneutic (*Verbum Domini* 35-39).

In the Protestant world there is also much energy around this recovery of the Word. A recent survey by the Centre for Bible Engagement, which polled 40,000 people, found that the lives of people who engaged Sacred Scripture four times or more a week were significantly different from those who did so only once, twice or three times a week. People who read Scripture most days of the week have experienced dramatic change in many areas of their lives: feeling lonely drops 30 per cent; anger issues drop 32 per cent; bitterness in relationships falls by 40 per cent; alcoholism drops 57 per cent; feeling spiritually stagnant drops 60 per cent; viewing pornography declines by 61 per cent; sharing the faith jumps 200 per cent; and discipling others jumps 230 per cent. (Zander Crauwcamp)

Encountering Christ through Scripture is a life-changing experience. I invite you to pick up your Bible and experience this invitation to deep transformation; not just in preparing a homily, but also as a vital part of your discipleship.

CHAPTER 2

A MYSTICAL UNION WITH CHRIST

Each type of homily has its place in history and in the toolkit of the preacher. The New Advent Encyclopaedia says the Greek word *homillia*, is best translated as, "to hold intercourse with a person", as used in 1 Cor 15:33 and Lk 24:14.

The word, therefore, has a nuptial implication. The homily is not a decree, a telegram, a fax, an email or a WhatsApp message. It is primarily about intimacy and person-to-person communication.

From the start, the homily has been associated with the Eucharist, as it explored Sacred Scripture and assisted the Christian in understanding the meaning of the Christ-event. The conversation of Jesus and the two disciples on the road to Emmaus demonstrates this: "And beginning with Moses and all the prophets, he explained to them what was said in all the Scriptures concerning himself" (Lk 24:26–27). There we have the first homily, open to encounter and connected with the Eucharist.

The early Church had several kinds of homilies. I will focus on three: **expository**, **hortatory** and **mystagogical**. Each of these contributes to the life of the disciple in a significant way.

The **expository homily** is the most common. It focuses on the text as text, interpreting it on the basis of the scriptural context, Tradition and the Christ-event. The aim here is to assist the congregation to come to knowledge and understanding of a dimension of the Scripture, or doctrine, showing how it illuminates the Christ-event.

The expository was my tried and tested method in my early years as a preacher. I would preach on the text and explore the inner connections within the text. I read the best commentaries and understood textual variants and sought to explore the text as text and demonstrate its beauty. When I was the Bishop of St Vincent and the Grenadines and Bishop of Barbados, I also used this form of homily frequently. In both dioceses the Catholic Church is a very small minority in a Protestant ocean.

The presumption of most Christians in those dioceses, was that Catholics were not really Christian. Because of this perception I would often explore a key mystery of faith to communicate the deep connections between the Scripture and the living tradition of the Catholic faith. On feasts of Mary, or of the apostles, or when the Scripture pointed to a key dimension of the Catholic tradition, I would seek to expose the truth in a way that the listeners could hear and understand. Pastorally this was vital, as 1 Peter says: "Always be prepared to give an answer to everyone who asks you to give the reason for the hope that you have" (1 Pet 3:14).

The **hortatory homily** seeks to move beyond text as text and points to the moral and spiritual wisdom contained in the text. Here the preacher aims to instruct so the listener may find deeper reasons for spiritual and moral action or conversion of heart. The hortatory homily points to spirituality and morals. We might consider it an upgrade from exposition; it takes expository discourse to the next level.

The hortatory form is also vital for giving moral instruction at a difficult or tense time. St John Chrysostom, when threatened by Empress Eudoxia, preached on the power she did not have, and the power Christ had. It pointed the congregation to where true power lies. Speaking truth to power should only be engaged when you are sure it is God who wants you to speak the specific word. In these situations, ego can entice and blind the preacher. This is a distraction to God's word. This type of confrontation should only be pursued after a clear discernment process and if possible, with someone else whom you trust.

As priest I preached the homily for the opening of the law court one year. The day before, a gang leader was killed. It was clear to me the orders for the killing came from a level higher than the gangs. The car used for the hit was burnt so DNA could not be retrieved. The killers were clearly professionals who operated in a very different way from the gangs. In the homily I made a comment linking the injustice in our nation with the killing of the gang leader. In my years working with the gangs, I had not encountered a case of murder by professional killers. Something in the underworld was changing and I felt compelled to speak to it. There was a firestorm and, let's just say, the Minister of National Security sent police to interrogate me later that week. There is always a price.

As priest and as bishop, and now as archbishop, I have preached on the thorny issues of the day. I have challenged politicians, prime ministers, civil authorities and the business community on different issues. Each time, there is a price to pay. This is why it is important that you are not on an ego trip, why it is important that you truly believe it is God's word you are preaching, that you approach this type of homily with purity of heart.

The **mystagogical homily** seeks to initiate the congregation into the sacred mysteries. It aims at the heart and seeks to invite the listener into the place where Christ is encountered. The aim of this form of homily is to lead the congregation to an encounter with Christ. Here Christ, by inviting the disciple to nuptial union, opens that person to a new dimension of faith. This level of encounter is available to all disciples.

Aristotle identified three characteristics of a speech: *logos*, *ethos* and *pathos*. A good speech needs balance and has all three. *Logos* refers to soundness of ideas and the veracity of the thoughts communicated (expository homily). This is vital if the homily is to be trusted and if it leads the hearer to the place of readiness for the encounter. *Ethos* speaks to the believability or trustworthiness of the preacher, the spiritual wisdom he is capable of communicating and the ethical life to which he is witnessing (hortatory homily). *Pathos,* on the other hand, speaks to the connection and intimacy that the homily invites the listener to enter into. Here we can now see the goal of the homily is to lead the congregation to nuptial union with Christ.

A Mystical Way

The homily, if treated well, is laid upon *logos* as its foundation, with *ethos* as its body and *pathos* as its beating heart and invites the congregation to an encounter with Christ. In this way the homilist moves beyond the text as text to the spiritual wisdom contained in the depth of the text. And just when you may be satisfied with leading the congregation into spiritual depth and wisdom, with offering a different perspective of a moral person and on making moral choices, just then, the homily, through God's grace transcends text and wisdom and leads to the encounter with the living God – *pathos*. It is this encounter with the living God that is the ultimate aim of the homily. I believe we need a new expectation from the homily – the birth of the word of God in the soul of the preacher and the hearer of the word (mystical encounter).

Karl Rahner the renowned German theologian, said: "The Christian of the future will be a mystic or he will not exist at all." This is a serious and significant statement. The mysticism that Rahner speaks about is not an esoteric teaching given to the few. It is at the very core and centre of Christianity, in which all disciples are invited to participate. It is the mysticism of ordinary everyday life; about "finding God in all things", as St Ignatius would say.

The expectation is that every baptised disciple of Christ would come to mystical union. Not some, but all! William Blake captures this in the opening of his poem *Auguries of Innocence:*

To see a World in a Grain of Sand
And a Heaven in a Wild Flower
Hold Infinity in the palm of your hand
And Eternity in an hour

I believe the challenge we face with the Mass today is that we have not initiated our people into the sacred mysteries. We have not given them the expectation to have mystical union with Christ. We have not gone beyond the text as text, or the text as spiritual wisdom, to the text as invitation or portal into the sacred mystery that is Christ.

Christ Life

In his 2013 encyclical *Lumen Fidei*, Pope Francis commenting on a dialogue between the martyr Hierax and the Roman prefect Rusticus, said: "For those early Christians, faith, as an encounter with the living God revealed in Christ, was indeed a 'mother', for it had brought them to the light and given birth within them to divine life, a new experience and a luminous vision of existence for which they were prepared to bear public witness to the end" (5).

The birth of the Word of God in the soul of the preacher and then in his hearers is the ultimate aim of preaching today. Don't get me wrong: we need good expository preaching to ensure our people have the foundations of faith and a firm grasp of the Scripture as sacred text.

We also need preaching that points to spiritual wisdom and speaks to the will, opening the depth of the Tradition to our people. But, for the Church in the 21st century to be truly alive and be the body of Christ in the world today, we need mystagogical preaching to initiate our people into the sacred mystery that is Christ.

In mystagogical preaching, the Word is born anew in the soul of the hearer. This Christ Life, this life of grace that is conceived, bears a marvellous harvest of discipleship. This is how the Church renews itself constantly.

CHAPTER 3

THE HOMILY GIVES MEANING TO THE WORD

The homily is an integral part of the Liturgy of the Word. Through the homily, the preacher explores the Sacred Scripture given for the day. The intention is to make the sacred text clear and to give its meaning. This is both an art and a science.

Nehemiah

In Nehemiah 8 we see this clearly. The Levites instructed the people gathered before them in the square. They read from the Book of the Law of God, making it clear and giving the meaning so that the people understood what was being read (7,8).

The Bible is a library of books, each one having a different way of conveying its message. In your library you do not read the comics the way you read a history book or a novel. You know and understand the type of book (literary genre) you are reading. With the Bible it is important for the hearer of the Word to understand the genre to gain a clearer sense of the text.

Nehemiah speaks both of making it clear and giving the meaning, and so to reveal the sacred mystery. This is at the heart of the homily: to lay bare the sacred mystery and invite people to enter into an encounter with Christ.

Nurturing the Christian life

On the homily, the *General Instruction of the Roman Missal* says:

> The homily is part of the Liturgy and is highly recommended, for it is necessary for the nurturing of the Christian life. It should be an explanation of some aspect of the readings from Sacred Scripture or of another text from the Ordinary or the Proper of the Mass of the day and should take into account both the mystery being celebrated and the particular needs of the listeners (65).

This is a very rich text. The necessity of the homily is for "nurturing the Christian life", a wonderfully loaded phrase. In Genesis 2:15, Adam is given the priestly mandate – to till and to guard. It is translated differently in some versions of the Bible, e.g., to subdue, which changes the clarity and the meaning. Till and guard is what a gardener does. To till is to nurture, to turn up the soil and make it ready to receive good seed. To guard is to protect from harm, both external (thieves) and internal by overgrowth of plants or weeds, thus weeding and pruning.

The homily needs to nurture, weed and prune to ensure Christ Life flourishes in the heart of the listeners. Christ Life is that life of grace we received at baptism. It is the most precious gift we have ever received which, if nurtured well, will lead to sanctity and eternal life. This is the purpose of the homily: to inspire the Christian to sanctity and to prune and weed, ensuring the conditions for growth (cf. 2 Tim 3:16).

Focused on the Word

The next part of the text is important. There are only three things on which the preacher can focus: the Scripture read for that day, the feast, or text of the Liturgy. This is vital! We are a lectionary people. We are given the text of the day and we believe God speaks through that text or feast to the people. The homily is meant to explore the sacred text, making it clear and giving the meaning. The only exception is on the occasion of a feast, when the Proper of the Mass can be the focus.

This is a sacred task. The challenge for the preacher is to chew the Word till it speaks to him, till it comes alive in him and is no longer words but a portal to the Word who became flesh and dwells among us.

In *Joy of the Gospel*, *Evangelii Gaudium* (EG), Pope Francis says: "Whoever wants to preach must be the first to let the word of God move him deeply and become incarnate in his daily life. In this way preaching will consist in that activity, so intense and fruitful, which is 'communicating to others what one has contemplated'" (150).

This requires deep preparation both immediate and remote. The Holy Father says: "Preparation for preaching is so important a task that a prolonged time of study, prayer, reflection and pastoral creativity should be devoted to it" (EG 145). It is a serious defect to turn up for the

Sunday liturgy unprepared or under-prepared. It is the pivotal moment of the week for priest and people.

Francis Chan, an Evangelical megachurch pastor, said recently he never knew that for 1500 years all Christians believed the Eucharist was the real presence of Jesus. It was the Protestant Reformation that moved the Eucharist (Jesus) from the centre, giving emphasis to the lectern and men's ideas.

Catholic preaching is focused on the Scripture given to us through the Lectionary. The preacher chews that Word till it penetrates him, then he can give it to the people. The homily is not about the ideas of the priest, or the latest book he read, or pet peeve he has. It is about Jesus Christ speaking to His people through the particular text. Our job is to make it clear and give the meaning.

When the preacher prepares well, the people are initiated into the sacred mysteries where they encounter Christ. The mystery and the needs of the people are paramount. Thus, the preacher needs to know his people, to know how to move them to the next step of the journey. He must also have experienced the mystery to lead his people to the sacred encounter.

CHAPTER 4

DIVINE INTERCONNECTION – WORD AND EUCHARIST

The *General Instruction of the Roman Missal* 65 says the homily is necessary for nurturing the Christian life. St Ignatius of Loyola speaks about Christ-life as the life of grace that we were given in baptism when we were grafted into Christ. The homily is necessary for nurturing this life. For Christ Life to flourish, we need eyes to see Christ, encounter him, and follow him in his mission.

Centrality of the Cross

On the road to Emmaus (Lk 24:13–35) the Christian theology of the homily is laid out before us. The text is rich, with many layers. The disciples were distraught and fleeing Jerusalem in despair when the stranger walked up to them. They recount their hopes, broken dreams and disbelief to him. What unfolds next is pure grace and mercy.

After he chides them for being foolish and slow, the companion gives them the principle for interpreting Scripture, "Did not the Messiah have to suffer these things and then enter his glory?" (Lk 24:26)

Two challenges stump them. First, like Peter and the apostles in Matthew 16:22–23, they could not comprehend a suffering Messiah – had no capacity for seeing suffering as redemptive. This was the first block to the message of the Resurrection.

Second, they could not believe a dead man could come back to life. The first thing Christian preaching must do is address these two blocks. If we cannot see suffering and the cross as redemptive, we will not be prepared to suffer and die for Christ. If we do not believe in the Resurrection, there is no ground or hope for our faith: We will live rather to preserve our life in this world, and thus lose our soul (Mt 16:24–25).

St Paul says he resolves to know nothing except Christ and Christ crucified (1Cor 2:2). The cross of Christ is central to nurturing Christ Life. The Resurrection is the portal that allows that life to come alive in us.

Interplay of the Old and New Testament

Then, "beginning with Moses and all the Prophets", the companion explains to them, "what was said in all the Scriptures concerning himself" (Lk 24:27). Part of the spirituality of the lectionary is that the Old Testament reading is chosen specifically to interpret and shed light on the New. We read the events of Jesus, and understand their meaning, through the lens of the Old Testament. This is central to understanding the homily.

Jesus, "beginning with Moses", interprets the Old Testament to show that the Christ should suffer and die to enter into his glory. We cannot get to glory except through the cross, just as we cannot understand the Jesus event except through a reading and interpretation of the Old. Cross and glory must both be held.

Portals to Mystery

Just as we interpret the New Testament in the light of the Old, we interpret the breaking of the bread through the breaking of the Word. They are interconnected.

The text continues: "When he was at the table with them, he took bread, gave thanks, broke it and began to give it to them. Then their eyes were opened, and they recognised him, and he disappeared from their sight" (Lk 24:30, 31).

In the Resurrection appearances there is a familiar pattern. The disciples see a stranger whom they do not recognise. Some interaction follows, and then they recognise him. For Mary it was being called by name (Jn 20:16), with Thomas it was touching the wounds of Christ (Jn 20:24–29), with Peter it was the abundance of fish (Jn 21:7ff), at Emmaus it is the breaking of the bread.

These portals to mystery are not for the original disciples alone; they are structures of grace and allow us in. We too can see Jesus in the breaking of the bread.

Open Eyes

Apostolic Nuncio Archbishop Fortunatus Nwachukwu makes a wonderful point here. In the Book of Genesis, Eve is seduced by the promise that by eating the fruit "your eyes will be opened, and you will be like God, knowing good and evil" (Gen 3:5).

This is the subtlety of evil; what is promised is very different from what happens. After eating, "the eyes of both of them were opened, and they realised they were naked; so they sewed fig leaves together and made coverings for themselves" (Gen 3:7). Their eyes were opened but only to see themselves. Thus, they realised they were naked and were ashamed. The sin moved their eyes from God to themselves causing shame.

In the Emmaus story we have the reversal. The disciples' eyes were opened (Lk 24:31) and again they saw the Lord. Spiritual sight was restored, they were no longer looking at themselves. They recognised Christ. This is the fruit of the encounter with the resurrected Christ – we move our gaze from ourselves to God.

Burning Hearts

With their eyes opened, they ask each other, "Were not our hearts burning within us while he talked with us on the road and opened the Scriptures to us?" (Lk 24:32) In the breaking of the bread, the disciples realised what was happening within them. An inseparable connection exists between the breaking of the Word and the breaking of the bread.

Before their eyes were opened, they were not aware their hearts were burning. Without the breaking of the Word, they would not have been ready to encounter Christ in the Eucharist. Without the Eucharist they would not have realised their hearts were burning. Word and Eucharist need each other for the disciple to enter through the portal to the sacred mystery. This is how Christ Life is nurtured.

The "General Introduction" to the *Roman Missal: Lectionary* states:

The purpose of the homily at Mass is that the spoken Word of God and the liturgy of the Eucharist may together become a proclamation of God's wonderful works in the history of salvation, the mystery of Christ. Through the readings and homily Christ's Paschal Mystery is proclaimed; through the sacrifice of the Mass it becomes present. Moreover, Christ himself is also always present and active in the preaching of his Church (24).

CHAPTER 5

UNDERSTANDING THE SACRED MYSTERIES

A mystery is something we enter into, through which we encounter the living God. It is pregnant with meaning and invites the person into the encounter with Christ. This is not something we do: it is a path to encounter God. It is to be plunged into something so big, our finite minds cannot contain it.

We begin the Mass with the Sign of the Cross. Here, we are plunged into the mystery of the Trinity. God is one, yet God is three. The desire of this God – Father, Son and Holy Spirit – is that we may have life and participate in His divine life.

Immediately after we sign ourselves, the priest says: "Let us acknowledge our sins, and so prepare ourselves to celebrate the sacred mysteries." Words matter! This opening line of the Mass reminds us that what we are celebrating *are* **sacred mysteries**. This is an ancient term with much meaning.

Hidden Mystery

St Paul, in his letters to the Corinthians and Ephesians, speaks about the hidden mystery: "Surely you have heard about the administration of God's grace that was given to me for you, that is, the mystery made known to me by revelation, as I have already written briefly" (Eph 3:3, 4).

The apostle, as we know, encountered Jesus Christ on the road to Damascus. In that meeting his life was transformed deeply, and he was given a different path. Remember, after the encounter he became blind. Only when Ananias prayed for him did the scales fall from his eyes and his sight return.

St Paul lays bare the sacred mystery in Ephesians 3:6, saying this mystery is that through the gospel the Gentiles are heirs together with Israel – members together of one body, and "sharers together in the promise in Christ Jesus".

This is the heart of the mystery, we who were outside of God's grace have received grace in abundance. We are invited to be children of God and partakers in the mysteries that were available only to the Jews. We are integrally connected to each other through Christ. St Paul uses "mystery" to refer to the whole message of salvation that is now revealed to the Gentiles – that is to us. We are now invited to participate fully in the divine life of grace.

Mystery and Sacrament

The Catechism of the Catholic Church 1131 defines a sacrament as an "efficacious sign of grace, instituted by Christ and entrusted to the Church, by which divine life is dispensed to us" through the work of the Holy Spirit. The sacraments (called 'mysteries' in the Eastern Churches) are seven in number.

The Catholic Bible Dictionary notes: Scripture does not use the word "sacrament". Rather, the term was adopted by ancient theologians to describe the defining actions of Christian worship. In referring to a sacrament, the Western Church used the Latin term *sacramentum*, meaning "oath", whereas the Eastern Church utilised the Greek term *mysterion*, meaning "mystery". It is sometimes said that the Latin expression highlights the exterior dimension of a sacrament as a sign of grace, whereas the Greek expression stresses the hidden, interior action that takes place when a sacrament is administered.

But the ancient Church spoke about mysteries in a way that is different from the way we speak about sacrament today. For the modern mind, a sacrament is something we do, a religious rite we accomplish. This is a great failing of our process of initiation and religious formation. I believe we need to return to mystagogical preaching if we are to initiate our people into the sacred mysteries where they can live full active and conscious participation in liturgy and life.

Initiation

This loss of understanding the language has diminished the expectation of the Catholic, dulled the experience, and deadened the sensitivity of those leading the ritual and those participating in it.

In the ancient Church, the bishop and the priests were considered *mystagogues*, persons who initiated others into sacred mysteries. This older understanding of the sacrament as a sacred mystery, into which one needed to be initiated, is vital for our day.

The tool for initiation into the sacred mystery is myst-agogical preaching. Read the homilies of St Ambrose or St Cyril. Craig A. Satterlee, in *Ambrose of Milan's Method of Mystagogical Preaching,* defines mystagogical preaching as "… sustained reflection on the Church's rites of initiation, preaching on the 'mysteries' of the Christian faith". Also, he says, the goal of such preaching is "the formation of Christians rather than providing religious information to Christians" (2).

What are we to make of the many Catholics who do not live their faith; the many who believe the Mass is an obligation or boring; who go to Mass regularly yet do not act like Catholics in their families or in the public sphere? My best explanation is that they were not initiated into the sacred mystery. They were not offered a solid diet of mys-tagogical preaching. If we do not understand or expect the sacrament to yield to this sense of mystical encounter, we will not be prepared for, or expect the encounter with Christ in the sacraments. We would not understand the role of the Holy Spirit in the lives of the disciple. Nor would we understand discipleship.

It is especially in, and through the homily, that the priest initiates the people into the sacred mystery.

In the early Church, people were not given the full understanding of the mystery of Christ until they were fully initiated. It seems to me we are baptising and catechising and *sacramentalising*, but we are failing to initiate our people into the sacred mysteries where they have a vital connection with the Trinity – Father, Son and Holy Spirit.

What if you used the full Lent and Easter season for mystagogy? What if you did your work, read the ancient homilies and understood how to connect the Sunday readings to mystagogical preaching that reaches the heart, mind and imagination of your people?

Sacred Mystery

Mystagogy is not an esoteric branch of Christianity reserved for the few. It is initiation into the mystery of Christ, which is open to all who desire to live their lives fully in Christ. This is what St Ignatius speaks about in his phrase, "finding God in all things". This is not secret knowledge to which only a few will have access. It is about knowledge given to all for the sake of all, to bring broken humanity to encounter Christ, that we may be joined into Christ as a branch to a vine, or a member to its body.

This is not a competition between the heavenly and the earthly. It is rather about having the eyes to see the intersection of these two in every moment and every place. We come to Mass to enter into the sacred mystery, through which we encounter Christ who is present to his Church and in his world. This is the sacred task of the preacher, to initiate the people of God into the sacred mystery and help them gain eyes to see God who is present in all things.

CHAPTER 6

AN EAR TO THE PEOPLE[1]

Calling the Congregation to Full, Conscious, and Active Participation through the Sunday Homily

The preacher must know the heart of his community, in order to realise where its desire for God is alive and ardent, as well as where that dialogue, once loving, has been thwarted and is now barren.

(Francis, *Evangelii Gaudium* 137)

Introduction

As a seminarian I was assigned to assist an elderly priest with his Sunday Mass at the Cathedral. The priest had suffered a stroke many years before and lost his eyesight. My role was to stand by his side and read the text if he forgot the next words. He had memorised the Mass but could get distracted. My second task was to preach the homily since he could not.

On the first Sunday, I woke up with a very queasy stomach. It was bad. I could not think of what I ate the night before, but I ensured I knew where the little room was and how to get there if necessary. I survived the ordeal and managed to escape without incident.

---

[1]This was first given as: The Carl J. Peter Lecture. North American College, Rome Lent 2017

The next Sunday to my shock the same thing happened. It was not what I ate, it was my nerves and anxiety about preaching. I felt unprepared, overwhelmed and had massive anxiety. I was not a natural homilist; preaching did not come easily to me! For the first five years of priesthood, every weekend I struggled bitterly with the text to find a word from God for the people. For me preaching was, is and continues to be a difficult task.

A Call

If preaching was not a call, I would not speak in front of large audiences. I would not bear the ordeal of preaching. Yes, it is an ordeal!

The apostles were first called to companionship and preaching (Mk 3:14). To this call, before his death, Jesus added keeping his memory alive (Eucharist). After the Resurrection, he gave them power to forgive sins (Jn 20:23) and the Great Commission: "Go into all the world and preach the gospel to all creation" (Mk 16:15). Here the key elements of apostolic life are established and handed on to the bishops and then to the presbyterate. Preaching is integral to our vocation and to the mission of the Church.

St Paul speaking about his right to financial support by the community, makes some interesting comments about preaching: "For when I preach the gospel, I cannot boast, since I am compelled to preach. Woe to me if I do not preach the gospel! If I preach voluntarily, I have a reward; if not voluntarily, I am simply discharging the trust committed to me" (1 Cor. 9:16). For St Paul preaching is not an optional extra, it is integral to his vocation. It is an obligation to which he is compelled.

At the opening of his public ministry in the Gospel of Matthew, Jesus preaches repentance for the Kingdom of Heaven (Mt 4:17) In Luke's Gospel when he unrolls the scroll of the prophet Isiah to read, Jesus gives us a glimpse into his understanding of the mission entrusted to Him: "The Spirit of the Lord is on me, because he has anointed me to preach good news to the poor" (Lk 4:18). Here we learn that preaching good news is a work of the Holy Spirit and it is integral to Jesus's identity and his mission.

If we imagine a toolkit for building the Kingdom, preaching is one of the tools most frequently used by Jesus, the first apostles and the early Church. As Jesus connects preaching to the Holy Spirit (Lk 4:18), St Paul connects it to the Cross of Christ, "…but we preach Christ crucified: a stumbling block to Jews and foolishness to Gentiles, but to those whom God has called, both Jews and Greeks, Christ the power of God and the wisdom of God" (1 Cor 1:23).

This sets the backdrop for speaking about the importance of preaching in the life of the Church today. The Sunday homily is the most used tool in the priest's toolkit. It gives the pastor the greatest opportunity to reach and form most of his people most consistently. However, I fear it is not always used well or appropriately.

When used well, preaching allows a pastor to bring renewal to his parish and to engage his people in stewardship and participating in the life of the Church. Preaching opens the community to the sacred mystery of Christ amongst us in the sacraments and the poor; it is how the priest connects people with their vocation and provides the pathway and tools to achieve our ultimate purpose – holiness.

Yet, preaching is the single most taxing responsibility of the priest. It certainly keeps me on my knees in humble receptivity as I search through the text and commentaries, listening and waiting for the word that God is proposing to his people for that day.

Preaching with Vision

In *Alice in Wonderland*, the classic penned by Lewis Carroll, Alice came to a crossroad and saw a cat and asked, "Sir, which of these roads should I take?" The cat replied, "It depends on where you want to go." Alice said: "I don't really know." Then said the cat, "It really does not matter which road you take, each one would be as good as another."

Vision is an aspiration for your community that creates a path from the present situation to a future state. For Jesus, his vision was the Kingdom of God; he proclaims it at every opportunity possible.

Stephen Covey in his *Seven Habits of Highly Effective People* articulated the Second Habit in this way: begin with the end in mind. Before we can begin preaching, we need to know God's intention for the community. From this perspective, preaching is pointing out the signposts and facilitating the community along the journey to the Kingdom of God. Without a clear vision for the community, the Sunday homily will be a series of hit-and-misses that people will either enjoy or endure; it will entertain or bore, but it will not assist the People of God to make their journey to holiness in a seamless and consistent way.

Every homily should therefore connect the congregation with both the ultimate vision and the next step they need to take along their journey. Preaching is not about dazzling the congregation with an intellectual titbit you learned in seminary; it is about connecting God's people with their vocation through the Word and showing the next developmental step along their journey.

If you became pastor of a parish today what would you want for **your people**? This should keep you up at night on your knees wrestling with God. Think about it! What are the most important things you would want for **your people**? Put another way, what are the most important things God would want for God's people today?

Here is my list:

1. To hear God's call personally and find the courage to live it (vocation);
2. To be missionary disciples living with integrity and generosity (stewardship and evangelisation);
3. To become the best version of themselves (integral development); and
4. To be mystics having a deep interior life (mystical union).

It is my belief that if I were holy enough, if I listened more carefully to God's Word and preached every week in obedience to it, the People of God would be much further along this journey. The community would comprise missionary disciples fully alive in Christ serving the needs of all persons who are on the margins.

Regardless of the pastoral need or priority, regardless of the state of the community or its individual members, those in the pew or those who left the Church, the Sunday homily is the bridge between wherever the Church is today and the Church that God wants, tomorrow.

What would be your main strategy to increase participation in ministry? Or to increase the generosity of your people? Or to begin a new ministry? Or to help your people grow in moral virtue and holiness? The Sunday homily is the place where you have the greatest impact to achieve most of your pastoral priorities.

A pastor with a vision would spend between 12 and 20 hours a week on his Sunday liturgy. The Sunday Mass is where you meet your people, where you have the opportunity to form them, where you can lead them to the next stage of their development.

The *Homiletic Directory* published in 2014 by the Congregation for Divine Worship and Sacraments says, an effective homily requires prayer, preparation, knowledge of the people who will be in the congregation, a reflection on what is happening in the community and the world, and an invitation to the Holy Spirit.

Consider this. *The Pew Report* of August 2016 says 83% of people who are looking for a new church consider the quality of the homily as very important. Do you want to grow your church? Then the Sunday homily is vital. A

recent study of Catholic and Protestant clergy by *Pulpit &
Pew* finds, Catholic priests spend on average 16 hours per
week on the Sunday liturgy. This is 31% of their work
week. But please do not feel any pressure by these statistics
or you may have the same experience of my first homily!

Challenges of the Preacher

Before preaching, I try always to be conscious of this
one Question: **Who is speaking to whom?** Is it I speaking
to the people in front of me? Or is it Christ speaking to
God's people through me? If Christ is present in his Word,
then I am a conduit through which the Word comes to the
People of God, of which I am the first hearer.

Paul VI, in *Mysterium Fidei*, says:

In still another very genuine way, He [Christ] is
present in the Church as she preaches, since the
Gospel which she proclaims is the word of God, and
it is only in the name of Christ, the Incarnate Word
of God, and by His authority and with His help that
it is preached, so that there might be "one flock rest-
ing secure in one shepherd" (36).

Preaching is a function of Christ for the sake of His
Bride the Church, the priest enters into *persona Christi* as
he preaches. It is not my word, my intention, my brilliant
ideas or desire for the congregation that is vital and important. It is Christ's intention that we must seek out and proclaim. This is why preaching is the single most
exasperating activity of the priest – an activity that keeps

me on my knees. I cannot rest till I hear the Word of God that speaks clearly through the words of the text given for that day.

The **first and most difficult challenge** of the preacher is to listen deeply to the text given and find in this text what Christ is saying to his Bride the Church. As a young priest I began homily preparation by engaging the text through head and heart, listened to the text in prayerful meditation and listened to the text through reading the best commentaries I could find. I read until I understood the word, its inner dynamic and contradictions, its brilliance and challenge, the social significance of the actors, the core message of the text. The thing that God is doing in the text to the first hearers of the word; the thing that God is doing in and through the text today as I hear it and as it reads me.

This is both an intellectual and deeply spiritual engagement with the text. This is at the core of priestly spirituality. Pope Francis says: "Preparation for preaching is so important a task that a prolonged time of study, prayer, reflection and pastoral creativity should be devoted to it" (EG 145).

In the Catholic Tradition we have what I call the spirituality of the lectionary. Other ministers get to choose their text depending on what they want to say to their congregation that week. Catholic priests are given the text! For me this is a key element of the priest's spirituality. I believe God speaks in a specific and direct way to the community and its needs through the text that is given that day. For us there is a liturgical reading as there is an exegetical and divine reading of the text. The first reading on the Sunday, interprets the Gospel and points to how the Church seeks to interpret it.

As priests we need to learn to listen to and discover the Word of God that speaks to us through the text given to us by the Church. The Word is a person who invites us to an encounter, to conversion, to discipleship.

If you remember nothing else, remember this – Christ speaks today to his people in the concreteness of their lives and journeys, through the text that is given in the Lectionary. Our task and burden as priests is to hear through all the words, to the Word that wants to become flesh and dwell amongst us.

As Pope Francis says: "The homily has special importance due to its Eucharistic context: it surpasses all forms of catechesis as the supreme moment in the dialogue between God and His people which lead up to sacramental communion" (EG 137).

The **second most difficult challenge** about preaching is that it requires you to wrestle with God till the word overpowers you. Thus, the Holy Father points out: "For all these reasons, before preparing what we will actually say when preaching, we need to let ourselves be penetrated by that Word which will also penetrate others, for it is a living and active word, like a sword 'which pierces to the division of soul and spirit, of joints and marrow, and discerns the thoughts and intentions of the heart'" (Heb 4:12) (EG 150).

The **third most difficult challenge** is that your homily should only have one big idea. Only one! This big idea comes from your engagement with the text and God. It emerges through your struggle and prayer, your exegesis and *lectio divina*. But it must only be one big idea, or people will not remember. Searching the text, the wrestling and – hopefully – the surrender is to allow you to find the one big idea, the pearl of great price that God desires to communicate that week.

To find the big idea, start this prayerful wrestling on Monday, reading and praying with the text, reading the commentaries and seeking to hear God's Word through the words of the text. It is your pearl of great price, when you find it, sell everything else and communicate that and that alone. This pearl, Pope Francis reminds us, is best communicated through a sentiment and an image (EG 157).

Pope Francis says: "A preacher has to contemplate the Word, but he also has to contemplate his people...He needs to be able to link the message of a biblical text to a human situation, to an experience which cries out for the light of God's word" (EG 154). This is what I call the *dynamic of the text*.

I define the *dynamic of the text* as, **the encounter with the Word of God that speaks from the text, that if acted upon, challenges the preacher and the community to the next step towards authentic Integral Human Development – the development of each person, every person and each dimension of the human person**.

The *dynamic of the text* is finding the action in the text, that Christ wants to invite the congregation to take. It is something that is happening in the reading itself that jumps off the page and speaks to the heart of the community of faith. It often answers an existential itch that the community has or confronts a blindness that is hindering discipleship. It speaks eloquently to the heart and soul of the preacher and the congregation. It offers a developmental step towards missionary discipleship. It is often communicated in a sentiment and an image.

If you want to preach to the millennial generation (persons born between 1982 and 2004), and have them listen, you have to be this vulnerable before God. This generation does not listen to authority. They do not care what university or seminary you attended, far less what degree you graduated with. They want authenticity: do I see a man of God before me? If they do, then you have the privilege of being heard. To be heard consistently, you will need to communicate through an idea, a sentiment and an image.

I will now propose four questions to every would-be preacher. My advice is, **never go to the pulpit unless you can answer these questions honestly and clearly:**

1. What is Christ saying to his community through the readings we are given?
2. Why is this important?
3. What is one step Christ is asking the congregation to make towards fulfilling this word?
4. What is the one really big idea to be communicated?

When you can answer these questions, you are ready to begin pulling together the homily. To answer these questions, the preacher needs to be on his knees before God in humble submission. I often end up begging and pleading for the Word to be manifest. It is humbling! It leaves me vulnerable! It requires of me coming to that place of encounter where I am willing to surrender my will and ego to Christ. Like Jacob, I often wrestle with the Lord. Like Jacob I am often wounded by the wrestling. Like Jacob I often see the ladder and peek into the Heavenly liturgy. I pray that like Jacob I will end up obedient to God's Word.

In the essay Church, Paradox & Mystery, de Lubac quotes Dietrich Bonhoeffer:

> What is important when all is said and done is not what this or that churchman wants; all that need concern us is what Jesus wants ... [Too] often we place obstacles before the word of God ... when we preach our personal convictions and opinions, day in day out, and have little time left over to preach Jesus himself ... We must search to understand the immensity and richness of what is given us in Christ and discard the essential poverty and narrowness of our personal views and convictions ... It is only in a commitment without reservation to the demand of Jesus Christ for total obedience that the utter liberation is achieved that is the essential requisite for communion with him (Crossroads Initiative).

Conclusion

Preaching is a call from God to you. No one becomes a priest because he chose it. It is a sacrifice, a call, a response. As such the first initiative of the preacher is God's initiative. Because of this call we are obliged to seek God's vision for the people entrusted to us. We need to understand how God calls them, what God wants with them and their potential and path to holiness. This vision becomes the backdrop of the preacher's mandate, the landscape against which the word is shaped and formed. With this landscape as backdrop, the preacher listens to the text given to the Church for the particular Sunday and discerns the Word of God that speaks to the community, through all the words that are read.

The Sunday homily is born out of a profound engagement between text and preacher or rather, between Christ and his priest; an engagement that is at once, intellectual and spiritual. It is discovery and call; it is a matter of both obedience and passion. The homily is discovered through discernment. It is focused on the one big idea that is discerned through the text. It is filled out with story and exploration, with catechesis and biblical insight, with a call to a specific action and an expectation of a response.

The whole purpose of the homily is to facilitate the community in its call to full conscious and active participation in liturgy and life. Through answering the call, the disciple moves from one stage of the journey to another: from attending Mass to participating in Mass; from coming to church to participating in the life of the community; from disciple to missionary disciple. Fired with this sense of mission, the disciple understands clearly his or her vocation – to transform the family, the parish community and ultimately the world, through Christ's love. Thus, he or she participates in Christ's mission bringing his people to full life in Christ.

CHAPTER 7
BIRTHING AN EXPERIENCE

I have often said preaching is the most exasperating priestly experience. In this chapter I want to lead you into the experience from inside. I will take you through the steps of preparation that I did for a gathering of the Caribbean Church.

Some people sit and write a homily in one go. Then they go and preach. I agonise over the word till the Word becomes flesh so, in that moment, there is both agony and ecstasy. To gather my best thoughts about a scripture passage does not take too long. If I am asking the critical question – What does God want to say to this people about this text? Oh! That could be pure drama. The bigger the occasion, the more difficult the text, the further I am from alignment with the key message of the text, the greater the challenge.

In 2019, a Caribbean-wide Mission Congress took place in Trinidad and Tobago over six days, with 15 dioceses of the region participating. I was down to preside and preach at the closing Mass which was expected to attract a gathering of between 12,000 and 15,000 persons. This final day, with the Mass as its centrepiece, was to be the highpoint of the week's activity.

On the Tuesday, in Tobago, we had a full church of schoolchildren for an entire day. It went very well. On

Thursday another 10,000 schoolchildren gathered in Trinidad. Then, on Friday and Saturday, some 500 delegates from our region came together to reflect on the theme "Baptised and Sent" – the theme of the extraordinary mission month. All went very well.

Two feature talks and the Mass were scheduled on the Sunday. There was a problem. It was the 25th Sunday in Ordinary Time, Year C. That is a problem! It is in the middle of Luke's catechesis on wealth. It is a very hard teaching. The Gospel text, Luke 13:1-13, is cryptic at best or difficult at worst.

Two weeks before the event I sat and opened the Lectionary and read through the text for the day. My heart fell. It was an impossible text to preach, at the end of a week when the missionary mandate was being given to the Caribbean Church. I quarrelled with Jesus, "Could you not give a better text to rally your Church for missionary discipleship?" Of course, there was no answer.

To remind you, this is the text of the dishonest steward who was denounced to his master for being wasteful. He decided he was too weak to dig and too proud to beg so he marked down the amount the debtors owed his master. The master praised the dishonest steward's astuteness. Then the text went on to address attitudes to money and the choice between God and mammon. How do you preach this Gospel, calling a congregation of over 12,000 to become missionary disciples? I was unsettled and restless because I could not find a way. God's desire and God's word eluded me.

Spirituality of the Lectionary

The Catholic preacher is invited to the spirituality of the lectionary. We are invited to believe that the word given on a given day is the Word of God for that people on that occasion. The job of the preacher is to discover the Word, in the midst of the words we read. It has always worked for me even if I cannot see it in the beginning.

A spirituality of the lectionary also invites us to find, in the First Reading, the mind of the Church to interpret the Gospel. If it is difficult to find the word in the Gospel, then go to the First Reading as a hermeneutic key to unlock the Gospel. So, off to the First Reading I went. It was Amos 8:4-7. My anxiety grew.

Amos is one of the most direct of the prophets. He did not want to be a prophet and reluctantly he answered God's call. His critique of Israel was fierce. This text is a call to reckon with the First Commandment. The people tolerate the feasts and sabbath but cannot wait for them to finish to make money. Amos accuses them of corruption – tampering with scales and fixing prices to make great profits – and worst of all, sacrificing the poor on the altar of progress. But what does any of this have to do with missionary discipleship?

A Toolkit

In the readings I could find no light, no inspiration, no word from God to speak to the Caribbean Church. I sat with the texts, I put them into a *Word* document and read them over and over and over again. I did *lectio divina* with the text. I sat and prayed silently and lived with the text for several days. The week of the Congress had begun, and I could not find "a word". So, I went on with my other four talks for the week. On Wednesday I returned to the texts again. This time I opened my toolkit.

I have built up a significant toolkit over the years. First with printed books, now with digital copy. Three years ago, I subscribed to *Verbum*, a Catholic digital toolkit that provides serious tools for biblical and theological studies. All the papal documents and patristic writings, Council documents, the Canon Law and writings of theologians and spiritual writers can be found there.

I currently have about 1700 books in *Verbum*. An annual subscription to *Catholic Productions,* where Brant Pitre does a marvellous exposition of the text from a Catholic perspective, has also been of great value. His hermeneutic is based on one question: How would a first century Jew hear this text?

I started with Pitre, listened to his exposition of the text, understood its technical aspects and its relation to the First Reading and the Psalm. There was no light. No sense of a Word from God. No direction to speak to the Caribbean Church, which was gathering on Sunday.

I then turned to the most used commentaries in my toolkit. *Luke* by Pablo T. Gadenz. In addition to giving an exegesis of the text, he shows how the Fathers of the Church and Church writings interpret the text. Next, I consulted *Catena Aura: Commentary on the four Gospels, Collected out of the Works of the Fathers, Volume3: Luke.*

This also gives the history of interpretation of the text by looking at what the Fathers of the Church say.

I dug into both of these commentaries. Still all I found was a complex rational explanation of how the steward was really using his brilliance to win friends rather than trying to amass money. I also read another interpretation. Behind the text was the Law against usury. St Augustine saw the man as a cheat and a fraud but adds that the praise was "not because the servant cheated, but because he exercised foresight for the future". This became my hermeneutic key into the reading.

St Ephrem the Syrian was the one who opened the text for me. Speaking of the steward, he said: "He was praised, therefore, because, by means of that which was not his, he set about acquiring that which was to be his, namely friends and supporters." He then concludes: "Buy for yourselves, O Adam, those things which do not pass away, by means of those transitory things which are yours."

The text was becoming clearer: it was about an exchange of wealth – transitory wealth for true wealth. It was a question of what we believed true wealth to be – money or friends? Mammon or the Kingdom of God? But, somewhere in there was a hinge or suggestion about almsgiving. But it was just a suggestion. "I was seeing people, but they were looking like trees" (Mk 8:24).

Next I went to the passage again and this time used the exegetical guide and biblical word study in *Verbum*. I looked at the Greek and delved deep into the structure and syntax of the text. I went through the text, word by word, line by line. Only one thing emerged from my search. The word "wasteful" (*diaskorpizōn*) was used both in Luke 16:1, as a reference to the steward, and in Lk15:13, as a reference to the younger son.

It was already Saturday morning. I had read the text many times, prayed with it, mulled over it and read some of the best commentaries. I delved into the Greek and the meaning behind words to see if there was some hidden treasure. I sat in silence with it. But the Word had not yet been born in my heart. It was still words and ideas in a jumble in my mind.

On Saturday we learnt that a storm warning had been issued. Our event had been planned for outdoors. We made a decision on Saturday afternoon to move to another venue. I was distracted by logistics. It was Saturday night – 1000 things in my head – and I did not receive the Word as yet. I still had a jumble of words. I said to Mary, "He overshadowed you and you conceived the Word, help me to allow him to form the Word for his people in my heart." Praying the rosary, I surrendered.

A Birth

On Sunday morning I awoke, and the Word was alive and active in me. I call this the *dynamic of the text*. It is where the text acts on the preacher, inviting him to go deeper and to conversion. Entering into the *dynamic of the text*, the encounter with the word that becomes the Word, my mind and heart was convicted by the Word and the homily emerged: there are two kingdoms and people need to understand the difference. They cannot continue to hobble between them.

St Ignatius has an exercise on the "Two Kingdoms" that came to mind. Then St John Paul has a big idea that Benedict XVI used as a hermeneutic key – *the logic of the gift*. If Amos spells out the logic of the Kingdom of the world, then the Gospel speaks to the logic of the Kingdom of God.

On the one hand, is the pursuit of money, corruption, minimising holy days and the sabbath, and ultimately sacrificing the poor on the altar of progress. On the other, the logic of the gift: stewardship and being wasteful. The steward was denounced for being wasteful, then he became wasteful through forgiveness. He gave away much wealth to people who owed debts. This is a great description of the Father of the two sons. He too was wasteful. He squandered his property and then gave forgiveness that was unwarranted. It was not dishonesty that was praised. It was the prodigious nature of forgiving debt. We, like the Father of the two sons, and the steward need to be prodigious in forgiving debt. The text became alive.

This text could be approached from many perspectives. The preacher's main task is to ask: What does God want to speak to this congregation on this occasion? Then wait till this becomes clear.

Each time I am asked to preach, I feel like Jeremiah: "You have seduced me, Lord, and I have let myself be seduced; you have overpowered me: you were the stronger" (20:7 ff.). It feels this way because I am then engaged in the process of surrendering to God's will –

self-emptying – giving up what I believe is important and understanding the mind of God for this text, for this people on this occasion. This surrendering and allowing God to be God is the requirement for the birthing of the Word.

Dynamic of the Text

Earlier I defined the *dynamic of the text* as, "the encounter with The Word of God that speaks from the text, that if acted upon, challenges the preacher and the community to the next step towards authentic Integral Human Development."

The *dynamic of the text* is finding that action in the text that Christ wants to invite the congregation to take. It is something that is happening in the reading itself that jumps off the page and penetrates the heart of the preacher. It often answers an existential itch that the community has or confronts a blindness that is hindering discipleship. The invitation speaks eloquently to the heart and soul of the preacher and the congregation, offering a developmental step towards missionary discipleship. It is often communicated in a sentiment and an image.

The *dynamic of the text* or what the Book of Hebrews calls the double-edged sword which penetrates "even to dividing soul and spirit, joints and marrow", judging the thoughts and attitudes of the heart (Heb 4:12).

In the conversation between the preacher, the Word who is God and the community, the *dynamic of the text* emerges. What is the word that God wants to speak to this people? This needs discernment of spirits. This is not what

I want to say! It is rather finding what God wants to speak to God's people. This is fundamental. There are many things I could say from any text. But the only thing worth speaking is the word that God wants to speak.

Pope Francis, in *Joy of the Gospel* 146, says:

This attitude of humble and awe-filled veneration of the word is expressed by taking the time to study it with the greatest care and a holy fear lest we distort it. To interpret a biblical text, we need to be patient, to put aside all other concerns, and to give it our time, interest and undivided attention ... "Speak, Lord, for your servant is listening (1 Sam 3:9)".

Here is the thing. The Word is shy and will not emerge till the preacher is willing to surrender and become receptive. The Word must be conceived – every conception a virgin birth. Every virgin birth needs a fiat! This is the core and heart of the spirituality of the preacher.

We do the work, we pray, mull over the text, delve into the commentaries and the original language. It is God who overshadows and allows the Word to be conceived in the preacher. It is really all God's work (2 Cor 5:18). The job of the preacher is to stay before God till the word is conceived and born. Till there is a movement in the soul. Till there is an excitement and a sense of the presence of God speaking through the text. Not just ideas, but God speaking. Then, like Mary, the preacher must say: "Let it be done to me according to your Word."

As we have already seen, when the *dynamic of the text* emerges then there are four questions to ask:

The Four Questions:

1. What is Christ saying to his community through the reading we are given?

2. Why is this important?

3. What is one step Christ is asking the congregation to make towards fulfilling this Word?

4. What is the one really big idea to be communicated?

My Four Questions Answered:

1. *What is Christ saying to his community through the reading we are given?* Be prodigious with mercy.

2. *Why is this important?* This is the heart and core of discipleship.

3. *What is one step Christ is asking the congregation to make towards fulfilling this Word?* Find someone who owes you a debt of forgiveness and be wasteful with your forgiveness.

4. *What is the one really big idea to be communicated?* There are two kingdoms with two value systems and two very different logics. Only one leads to life – be prodigious with mercy.

Practical Steps

What are the practical steps the preacher takes in approaching the Word?

1. *Lectio divina* with others, if possible.

2. Delve into the Scripture; use the best tools available.

3. Sit before the Blessed Sacrament in silence or in Christian meditation.

4. Let the Word work on you, let it be born in you till you surrender to the Word.

5. Search for the *dynamic of the text.*

6. Let the word challenge you and act from within.

7. Reflect on the 4 big questions.

8. Write your homily.

9. Practice it before a mirror or video tape it.

10. Deliver it with no notes.

Mary Our Model

If birthing the Word is the metaphor of the preacher, then Mary is the model and prototype for the preacher. While we do all the active work to interrogate the text, we need to be equally disposed to the contemplative work, to allow God to do in us as preachers what God wants. This contemplative work is vital if the homily is to be more than information and ideas. It is vital if the Word is to be born. It is also vital if the preacher is to become a better vessel of the Word who becomes flesh and dwells among us.

It is tempting for preachers to perform and impress their congregation. This leaves the preacher as the star and the people dependent upon him. The model of birthing requires the active participation of all so the Word can be born in people's hearts, inviting them to discipleship, intimacy and conversion.

If the dynamic of birthing happened regularly, the role of the preacher will shift as the congregation grows into mature discipleship. The preacher will no longer be central to the community, Christ is. As members of the community grow and develop their relationship with Christ, they will put Christ at the centre of their existence. Here we have discipleship and, I dare say, the journey to sanctity. This is the ultimate end of all pastoral engagement.

St Paul expresses this so well in the Letter to the Ephesians 4:11-16:

> So Christ himself gave the apostles, the prophets, the evangelists, the pastors and teachers, to equip his people for works of service, so that the body of Christ may be built up until we all reach unity in the faith and in the knowledge of the Son of God and become mature, attaining to the whole measure of the fullness of Christ.
>
> Then we will no longer be infants, tossed back and forth by the waves, and blown here and there by every wind of teaching and by the cunning and craftiness of people in their deceitful scheming. Instead, speaking the truth in love, we will grow to become in every respect the mature body of him who is the head, that is, Christ. From him the whole body, joined and held together by every supporting ligament, grows and builds itself up in love, as each part does its work.

Conclusion

Waiting on the Word could be very frustrating. It is very humbling and disconcerting. But spiritually it is falling into the hands of the living God and trusting God to work and give a Word to feed His people. By moving the homily from my word to God's word the preacher also moves the focus from himself to God. This shift in focus is vital if we are to form a mature people who will pursue God on God's terms.

The big question is what is the point of the homily? If the answer is to lead the people to God, then God needs to be there from the beginning of the process. Here Pope Francis's words about the word are stunningly accurate: "Whoever wants to preach must be the first to let the word of God move him deeply and become incarnate in his daily life. In this way preaching will consist in that activity, so intense and fruitful, which is 'communicating to others what one has contemplated'" (EG 150).

We cannot give people what we do not have: nor can we take people where we have not gone ourselves. This is why the Holy Father says: "Preparation for preaching is so important a task that a prolonged time of study, prayer, reflection and pastoral creativity should be devoted to it" (EG 145).

Sit with the word, let it penetrate you deeply. Then, yielding your will to God's will, the Word will be born in you. And through you, the Word will be born in the hearts of God's people. This is how we move people from the benches to mission. This is how we initiate people into the sacred mystery. This is how we invite our people to deepen their relationship with Christ.

CHAPTER 8

PREACHING AS BIRTHING THE WORD?[2]

The Christian of the future will be
a mystic or not exist at all.

Karl Rahner

My aim in this chapter is to speak about the homily as a space where Christ is encountered. For this to become the norm, it is important – in a consistent manner – that we go beyond the engagement with the text as text and the foundation of the homily (information/*logos*). We also need to go beyond the notion of the text as spiritual wisdom, insight and challenge (practical wisdom/*ethos*). To be consistent, I believe we need a new expectation – the birth of the word of God in the soul of the preacher and the hearer of the word (mystical encounter/*pathos*).

In his Apostolic Letter *Instituting the Sunday of the Word of God*, Pope Francis says: "we need to develop a closer relationship with sacred Scripture; otherwise, our hearts will remain cold and our eyes shut, struck as we are by so many forms of blindness" (8).

Thus, the first preparation for preaching should not focus on the congregation, but rather on the preacher's

---

[2]This was first given as: The Annual John S. and Virginia Marten Lecture in Homiletics at St Meinrad Seminary, October 2019, 29th edition.

engagement with the text, so it speaks to his soul and births in him a renewed relationship with Christ. If this becomes the discipline and experience of the preacher, then in the Sunday homily, the Word will become flesh and dwell among us.

Our last three popes have made encounter central to the Christian mystery. Benedict XVI speaking about St Bernard of Clairvaux says:

> Being Christian is not the result of an ethical choice or a lofty idea, but the encounter with an event, a person, which gives life a new horizon and a decisive direction.

> For Bernard, in fact, true knowledge of God consisted in a personal, profound experience of Jesus Christ and of his love. And, dear brothers and sisters, this is true for every Christian: faith is first and foremost a personal, intimate encounter with Jesus, it is having an experience of his closeness, his friendship and his love. It is in this way that we learn to know him ever better, to love him and to follow him more and more. May this happen to each one of us! (Benedict, *Catechesis on St Bernard of Clairvaux*, 2009)

If encounter is the heart of discipleship, the **priest preacher** must first encounter the Word before he can preach it. This is rooted in an understanding of priest as missionary disciple, *mystagogue* and friend, and defender of the poor.

The modern person has been overwhelmed with information. To be heard, to invite to communion, the homily has to move beyond the head to the heart, the will, the understanding and ultimately give birth to Christ in the soul.

Karl Rahner speaks about Christianity today, as either being mystical or not at all. This mysticism is not esoteric or divorced from the cut and thrust of ordinary life. It is rooted in the Ignatian sense that we can find God in all things. Rahner proposes an ordinary mysticism where the mother, father, teacher, baker, manager and priest all have equal capacity to encounter the living God in the ordinary stuff of their lives.

God is present in all moments and in all interactions and in all occasions: discipleship is living in this truth. This requires eyes to see, ears to hear and hearts to perceive. God is in all things! The homily must speak to this. Whatever else it does it must communicate a world which is pregnant with God. A world where God is being born in every moment, in each interaction, in all places. St Paul reminds us, in Colossians 1: "In him all things were created… He is before all things, and in him all things hold together" (16-17).

We must have the eyes to see. We are like the two men on the way to Emmaus. They did not have the eyes to see the truth. God was with them, yet they were downcast and lacking hope (Lk 24). Thus, Jesus tells his disciples: "Abide in me, and I in you. As the branch cannot bear fruit of itself unless it abides in the vine, so neither can you unless you abide in me" (Jn 15:4).

The mystical way is not for some. It is for all of us. How do we get to depth? How do we create the expectation of consistent encounter as vital for priesthood and discipleship? How do we see the mystical way as the way that Jesus has called all disciples?

The Relationship Between the Preacher and the Word

What is the purpose of the homily? Is it to impress people about how much you learnt in seminary? How bright you are? Is it to inform them of some dimension of faith? Is it to expose the Scripture so people could have a deeper appreciation of it? Or, is it to lead people to an encounter with the Word who pitches his tent among us?

In my younger days as a priest, I saw the priest as "midwife of the word". In this metaphor God is the actor, and the priest patiently attends to the delivery of the Word as it is being born in the hearts of people.

Reflecting on this metaphor more recently, I recognise while it contains some intriguing elements, there are some inadequacies. The midwife is witness and facilitator. To be involved the midwife needs certain skills – timing and rhythm, observation and willingness. Midwifery is a messy business. It is engaged. It is vital, especially if there are complications. Yet the midwife is not directly or personally involved in the birthing process. It is outside of her. She was not present for the conception and she did not experience the elation of conception or the challenge of pregnancy. Skill and service is what she brings.

In his *Joy of the Gospel* 150, Pope Francis says, "we need to let ourselves be penetrated by that word which will also penetrate others, for it is a living and active word, like a sword 'which pierces to the division of soul and spirit, of joints and marrow, and discerns the thoughts and intentions of the heart' (Heb 4:12)". This is not midwifery. This is more intimate and involved. There is an expectation that the preacher is actively, and yes, intimately involved in the birthing of the word. It is not happening outside of him; it is happening in him and through him in a physical way.

My reflection led me to a new image – Mary. In that first birth, Mary was intimately involved. Yet the initiative was a divine initiative. God sent the Angel Gabriel with a message, a word. "You will conceive and give birth to a Son [the Word]". And, "the Holy Spirit will come on you, and the power of the Most High will overshadow you" (Lk 1:31-35).

St John, speaking about the same event, says: "In the beginning was the Word, and the Word was with God, and the Word was God... the Word became flesh and made his dwelling among us" (Jn 1:1,14). The Word, born through Mary, is not for Mary, but for the whole world.

Rather than midwife, the preacher is the one through whom the Word is conceived and born. The preacher is intimately involved in the process of the Word and the efficacy of that Word in the hearts of the congregation. There is an action that must happen in the preacher. It is not the same as reading the news or making an announcement. It is the Word being born in the preacher's heart, which allows the Word to be born in the hearts of all the faithful.

Motherhood of the Church

In "The Motherhood of the Entire Church", de Lubac, going back to the age of the Patristics, argues that the image of the Church as mother is not restricted to baptismal catechesis where the font has been seen, traditionally, as the womb of the Church. He says the motherhood of the Church is the essential metaphor for the growth and development of the Church and for every Christian:

> If, therefore, the Church is mother, each Christian also is or should be a mother. In his place, according to his own vocation, in union with all the others, he participates in the maternal function of the Church.

> It is first of all in himself that, through the action of this Church, the Christian gives birth and growth to the Word of God which he has received, from which he lives and which he makes bear fruit.

> The mouth of the Father has begotten a pure Word; this Word appears a second time, born of the saints. Constantly producing saints, it is also itself reproduced by its saints.

> Here originate the innumerable variations on the birth and growth of the Word of God in the soul that have multiplied ever since.

> (de Lubac, *Motherhood*)

Using the image of mother, we can now see the tradition speaking about Christian initiation and growth from this central metaphor – the birthing and bringing forth of the Word in our hearts and the hearts of others.

De Lubac speaks here of the mystical way that was very familiar to all the patristic writers. The expectation of Christian initiation and of growth in Christ is that the Word be born in the soul. He quotes St Francis de Sales, who says, "It is the good Jesus to whom we must give birth and produce within ourselves." In similar fashion, St John XXIII wrote in his 1962 Christmas message: "O Eternal Word of the Father, Son of God and Son of Mary, renew once again in the secrecy of souls the wonderful marvel of your birth!"

If we contemplate this image of motherhood, we will see our task of preaching in a new light. It will also require of us new methods of preparation and a new way of approaching the Word.

Approaching Scripture for Birthing

One of the great temptations for the preacher is to approach scripture looking for a word to preach on. It is a grave danger because this connection with the Word is first about delivery, finding something to say. It leaves no space or expectation for the process of birthing. This might be why there is a sterility in preaching today. The Word is approached with utility in mind – finding something to say. We are trying to have God on our terms. We have become functionaries who deliver. This is not God's way.

God calls the whole People of God to be mother and to birth the Word. And this requires that we begin with an openness to the Word and an expectation for the message (angel) to be proposed to us – for the Word to be conceived and born in our hearts and then in the hearts of the congregation.

A Catholic Imagination

In his book, *Christ and Apollo: The Dimensions of the Literary Imagination*, William F. Lynch SJ gives us some invaluable insights. Lynch looks at the difference between the gnostic and the Hebraic imaginations. The men of the **infinite** and the men of the **finite** (19). These two forms of imagination are in competition in our contemporary world and within Christianity. Many have tried to gain insight of God by grasping the infinite. This is against the incarnation where God becomes bone of our bone and flesh of our flesh – the finite. Lynch says:

> "No matter what form the vision takes, however, or what its final goal – whether that be beauty, or insight, or peace, or tranquillity, or God – the heart, substance, and centre of the human imagination, as of human life, must lie in the particular and limited image or thing" (20).

He names five attitudes to the finite. In the first four, the contact is less than required for birthing and incarnation. These attitudes are, analogously the attitudes that preachers have to the Bible.

1) **Exploiters of the real**: These preachers touch the biblical text lightly, seeking insight or tenuous mystical contact. The text is supposed to offer up its

treasure without affecting the preacher. This is a magical attitude. It is not Christian (24).

2) **Psychologism**: These preachers touch the text lightly, not for the sake of the text or arriving at the infinite or beauty or God, but for arriving at the self. Lynch says: "Their aim is to create states of affectivity, areas of paradise, orders of feeling within the self…Intensified or ordered subjectivity is the goal; again, the means are the exploitation, the manipulation, distortion, or reduction of the real." This approach will never make contact with the real (24). It reduces the Word to psychological wisdom.

3) **Double Vacuum**: These preachers touch the text lightly penetrating the text then recoil with judgment about the finite, with emotion, disgust, boredom or anger and fly in a second movement that is unrelated to the first and constitutes an act of rebellion and escape into a world of infinite bliss (25). They have disdain for the finite hence the recoil. An example of this is Karl Bath's theology.

4) **Facers of the Facts**: This is the existentialist approach. "The beautiful thing, say these facers of facts, is to accept the absurdity and limitation of reality with nerve, sincerity, courage and authenticity. They do not admit the validity of the leap back out of this earthly vacuum into some infinite realm which the third type of imagination makes" (26). For these preachers there is no infinite or transcendence. The brutal truth of human reality is all they have.

5) **The Generative Finite**: For these preachers there is a direct and causal relationship be-tween the finite and the infinite. There is "a narrow and direct path through the finite", this path leads through the full gamut of human experience, of human finiteness. It is only in this engagement with the finite, for its own sake, that insight emerges (27). But what is the relationship between the two? Here he says: "With every plunge through or down into, the real contours of being, the imagination also shoots up into insight, but in such a way that the plunge down causally generates the plunge up" (27).

The generative finite is the Catholic imagination. It is the *kenosis*, the self-emptying. It requires that the preacher plunges down into the full nature of the Word that is given, all its peculiarity and finiteness, its linguistic and textual uniqueness, its human and cultural interactions, the full depth of its claims and propositions. In this plunge down into the text in its finiteness there is a plunge up into insight and revelation and access to transcendence.

Elsewhere Lynch says:

We must go through, the finite, the limited, the definite, omitting none of it lest we omit some of the potencies of being-in-the-flesh. This does not mean that we should go through it violently, looking for a means to a breakthrough; that would be to try to accomplish everything at one stroke … we must literally go through it. And in taking this narrow path directly, we shall be using our remembered experience of things seen and earned in a cumulative way, to create hope in the things that are not yet seen (7).

If we apply Lynch to the process of preparation for preaching, then we need to develop a methodology. We cannot touch the text lightly and find an insight and wisdom and run with that. Or flee into the psychological. Or touch the text and get into a tirade about all the negative in culture and human existence. Or touch the text as if it is only finite with no access to the infinite.

The text becomes a sacred portal to the infinite when it is touched deliberately and deeply; when the enquirer is patient and willing to go through the full drama of the humanness of the text; when the preacher is willing to sit and watch and wait on the text to open to the infinite or transcendent; and when the preacher believes that the words of the text are a portal to the Word who became flesh and dwelt among us, he also understands there is no shortcut, no going over, under or around the finiteness of the text. It is through the stuff of the text that the birth of the Word comes. We must be patient and persistent and not be afraid to press and delve deeply into the stuff of the text. This is how insight, or Christ is born again and again in our hearts.

Preaching as Formation

This is a formation model of preaching. When a congregation encounters Christ regularly through the homily, they develop and grow in their relationship with Christ. This leads to discipleship, to disciples finding their path to holiness. It is essential that preaching engages them on their journey to holiness. As de Lubac, quoting Hippolytus, says: "The mouth of the Father has begotten a pure Word; this Word appears a second time, born of the saints. Constantly producing saints, it is also itself reproduced by its saints." This is a process of true education.

I would like to define education this way: "Education is the miracle by which a person truly becomes his/her own parent." To educate, then, is to "bring out" (*e-ducare*), "to give birth to the person" (Jose Noriega, "Introduction: Education and the Art of Living").

The preacher's job is not to pour knowledge into a person, into someone's head! It is drawing out of the person, giving birth to and giving the person the capacity to give birth to a new self, as the individual gives himself or herself as gift to God and others. It is a miracle. It is – in its depth and at its core – about transformation and the capacity we nurture in the individual for this rebirth. Preaching is about creating the capacity in the congregation for deep sustained inner transformation. Our congregations should be able, through our preaching, to become better and better versions of themselves.

Carl A. Anderson has an understanding of the education process that will be useful for the preacher. It is: "To reveal the human person, to embrace a horizon greater than the human person, and ultimately to form hearts, minds, and bodies to pursue our human destiny as beings on a journey to God."

The preacher's experience should be that of St Paul who says: "My dear children, of whom I am again in the pains of childbirth until Christ is formed in you…" (Gal 4:19).

Some References

- en.wikipedia.org/wiki/Expository_preaching

- www.ignatiusinsight.com/features2007/print2007/delu bac_motherhdchurch_apr07.html

- www.google.com/amp/s/beblesstified.com/2017/04/04/ 4-ways-to-tell-the-difference-between-preaching-a-per-formance/amp/

- www.encyclopedia.com/environment/encyclopedias-almanacs-transcripts-and-maps/biblical-exegesis-chris-tian-views

- www.samstorms.com/enjoying-god-blog/post/10-things-you-should-know-about-the-demise-of-exposi-tory-preaching

- www.newadvent.org/cathen/07448a.htm

CHAPTER 9

AUTHENTIC INTEGRAL HUMAN DEVELOPMENT

The preacher does not only preach content, there is a universe communicated through the homily. Have you ever realised how different preachers take fundamentally different approaches to different texts? Many people think the biggest challenge to the unity of the Church comes from other denominations. There are times when I have found more agreement with people of other denominations than with some Catholics. This has to do with both the stage of development and the fundamental belief about people and the world.

Do you believe that people are capable of growth and development? Put differently, do you believe you can "teach an old dog new tricks"? I am not sure about dogs, but humans are capable of learning new things at every stage of life. Science calls this neuroplasticity. It is the theory that the brain is capable of fundamental growth and development. The mural networks are capable of growth and making new connections, which happens at the level of the individual neuron but also of the whole brain through remapping.

Culture is built on practices that we can see, values that we can observe and beliefs that we cannot always see. Our beliefs act like a paradigm, they both focus what we see and also filter out what we do not see. It is important for the preacher and would-be preacher to ask themselves what they really believe about humanity. There is, I believe a Catholic way of seeing the world. This way has been called authentic Integral Human Development.

This form of development has been simplified into three interlocking ideas by author Matthew Kelly. We are all called: (1) to become the best version of our self; (2) to achieve this we commit to incremental growth (small steps); and (3) continually. In this view, to become the best version of ourselves is to become saints. This may sound simple, but it is not simplistic.

When you meet an addict, or someone in serious sin, or a community that is divided by hate, or a person living on the street, or a teen who is in rebellion, what do you do? Give up on them? Do you believe they are lazy, or stupid, or rebellious? This fundamental belief either calls forth incredible energy for growth or stunts them in their current state. People who believe the best about you get the best from you. People who look at you with eyes of prejudice or dismissal stunt you and your capacity to grow.

Catholicity

It is important that the preacher has eyes to see the potential for development in his congregation. When they see you, they must believe you judge them capable of growth and development. Reflect on your experiences when people saw you and your potential to grow. How did that affect you? Contrast that with how you felt when people looked down on you, thinking you incapable of anything.

This is not self-help; this is a fundamental Catholic principle that has been the touchstone of popes, evident in Paul VI's claim that "authentic Integral Human Development is the vocation of the Church" (*Populorum Progressio* 1967), a position reaffirmed by Benedict XVI, in his 2009 encyclical *Caritas in Veritate.*

Benedict XVI, who I consider one of the brightest theologian popes since St Gregory the Great, goes so far as to propose *Populorum Progressio* as the new *Rerum Novarum*, Leo XIII's encyclical which has been at the foundation of the Church's social teaching, commented on and celebrated for over 100 years. Benedict XVI sees authentic Integral Human Development as the hermeneutic key for all areas of the social question in our time. It is about the development of all peoples, of each person and every dimension of the person. This is the vocation of the Church, or what the Church is called to by Christ.

Commenting on Paul VI's vision, Benedict XVI says, "…the whole Church, in all her being and acting - when she proclaims, when she celebrates, when she performs works of charity – is engaged in promoting integral human development" (*Caritas* 11). In all areas of Catholic life, therefore, we are promoting integral human development. This is a huge claim and a whole new way of seeing the ministry of the Church. It is my belief that authentic Integral Human Development is the touchstone or "mark" of Catholicity for the 21st century.

Small but Significant Steps

In *Populorum Progressio* (20, 21), Paul VI lays out the steps: from less human conditions – the lack of material necessities, moral deficiencies and oppressive social structures – to the more human – the possession of necessities, victory over social scourges, growth in knowledge, increased esteem for the dignity of others, and towards the spirit of poverty and cooperation for the common good. And then, to even more human – the acknowledgement of supreme values, and of God their source, and faith a gift of God who calls us to share as sons and daughters in the life of the living God.

There is a continuum between poverty and sanctity. Each step, each effort, is an opening to God's Holy Spirit who graces us with the gift of conversion. Each step is at once a movement to God and a growth in humanity. This vocation of development must become the underpinning of all pastoral ministry. The homily is the place where we can, in the most effective manner, assist our people to open their eyes to the vocation of development. More importantly, it is how the pastor invites his people to make incremental steps every week towards holiness. The two extremes here are either demanding a giant leap that no one is capable of, or seeing your people as incapable of advancing from their present stage.

The Preacher First

The demand of development on the priest requires that he be a real human being. He must be on a path of development. He needs to bring everything before God – the good the bad and the ugly. He needs to stand naked before God in all of his poverty and shame, in his pride and arrogance, in his growing recognition of how far he is from the person God wants him to be. It is only in our weakness that God's grace works in and through us. St Paul discovered this when he prayed three times for the Lord to remove the thorn in his flesh. Three times the Lord responded, "My grace is sufficient for you, for my power is made perfect in weakness" (2 Cor 12:9).

When we stand before God's people in liturgy, we stand naked spiritually. We stand *in persona Christi* in the consummation of the marriage between Christ and his Bride, the Church. We do not even have a fig leaf to hide our shame. People know if we have the goods or not; if we are careerists or men of God. They know if we have depth or ambition; if we are pastors or bureaucrats. We cannot lead our people where we are unwilling to go. If we are not on a path of authentic development, we cannot lead our people adequately; our pastoring and our preaching will be defective.

"When preaching takes place within the context of the liturgy, it is part of the offering made to the Father and a mediation of the grace which Christ pours out during the celebration. This context demands that preaching should guide the assembly, and the preacher, to a life-changing communion with Christ in the Eucharist" (EG 138). Another way of speaking about life-changing communion with Christ in the Eucharist is to speak about authentic, integral human development - that you commit to becoming the best version of yourself; that you commit to becoming a saint.

The Inner Life

To become the best version of yourself you need a priest mentor, who can call you out and speak honestly and freely with you. If you think older priests have nothing to offer you, think again. Men become great priests because they are mentored by great priests.

It means having a spiritual director with whom you are absolutely honest and regular confession. It means having a group of priest friends to hang out with regularly. It requires commitment to reading deeply and broadly, not only on spirituality and theology, but about culture, on fiction, economics, history, social theory, technology, cosmology, gene theory and neuroplasticity. You need to keep current on all major movements influencing modern life and society.

Read widely on homiletics – not just Catholic writers – but by evangelicals and other ministers who have a flourishing ministry of preaching. Read about organising your ministries or your parish. Commit to ongoing formation, thinking and learning. Have an open mind. Be willing to learn and grow.

The preacher also needs an active prayer life: of course, the Divine office we have all committed to pray daily, the reading of Scripture and reflecting on the word, praying the rosary daily as Our Lady of Fatima asked. As a daily discipline, meditation is a great way for the active pastor to quiet before God and listen to the still small voice. Include the *Examen Prayer* which St Ignatius says will keep a busy person close to Christ, if done every day. Whatever the form, commit significant time to prayer. I have found an annual silent retreat most helpful in keeping me focused on God. Make commitments for your spiritual life; they will pay great benefits.

A student once asked me how long it takes to prepare for a homily? I asked, "a really good one?" He said, "Yes". I told him, "Between 15 and 25 years. A really good homily requires a person who has surrendered his life, aspirations and gifts to Christ. This takes work, commitment and time.

Your homily will be a reflection of the depth of your surrender to Christ. Nothing short of a relentless commitment to doing the journey of development is worthy of the People of God, or the Christ who called you.

CHAPTER 10
THE SOUL OF PREACHING

St Paul, speaking to the Corinthians identifies different degrees of spiritual maturity. This is important. I believe the goal of Christian preaching, as of the whole pastoral life, is to facilitate your congregation making small steps towards maturity in Christ. In your congregation you will have people at different stages of the spiritual journey. You need to be conscious of this in your preaching.

The homily of a children's Mass cannot be approached like the homily of an adult congregation. But what if the adults are also at different stages of the spiritual journey. To the Corinthians, St Paul says: "Brothers and sisters, I could not address you as people who live by the Spirit but as people who are still worldly – mere infants in Christ. I gave you milk, not solid food, for you were not yet ready for it. Indeed, you are still not ready. You are still worldly (1 Cor 1-3).

St Paul recognised two things here: (1) his people were of different stages of faith development and (2) you feed different spiritual food to people at different stages of faith development. This means the preacher needs to understand the congregation's level of faith development and feed them appropriately.

One of the greatest mistakes of young preachers is to give to the congregation everything they received in seminary – theology. Because the theology enthralled you does not mean it will be beneficial to your congregation. There are three questions that the preacher needs to wrestle with long and hard: (1) What do I want to give the congregation from these texts? (2) What does the congregation need from these texts? And, (3) What is Christ saying to his community through the readings we have been given?

Ultimately the third proposition is the most important. Usually, I need to go through the first and second propositions to arrive at the third. As a young priest I waxed eloquent with all the variants of the Greek text and their significance for interpreting the word. Fresh out of university and wanting to impress people with my learning, I overwhelmed the congregation with detail and nuance of the text. People took from it what they could and grew in an appreciation for the complexity of the text. To be honest they also grew in an appreciation that I was learned. It was ego driving the homily style.

When I settled into preaching it was easier to get a sense of the character of the congregation. I would begin with a dialogical style, and by call and response I would sense the need or level of development of the congregation. Then, I would pitch the homily towards that need or level of the congregation. Sometimes on a weekend I would have four Masses. While the readings and general approach were the same, I would have at least three different homilies in terms of emphasis and communication style.

The third question is the most troubling. This is the one that keeps me up at night: What is Christ saying to his community through the readings we are given? I have found that when the work of distillation is done well, this final question comes into clearer focus. Remember to answer these four questions:

1. What is Christ saying to his community through the readings we are given?

2. Why is this important?

3. What is one step that Christ is asking the congregation to make towards fulfilling this word?

4. What is the one really big idea to be communicated?

Answering these questions gets to the heart and core of the message to be communicated. From this point the message could be modulated to the needs of different congregations.

If we take the analogy of St Paul of some people being babies and others already adults, then we also see a developmental approach to preaching. For this approach, I have already articulated four stages:

1. To hear God's call personally and find the courage to live it (Vocation).

2. To be missionary disciples living with integrity and generosity (Stewardship and Evangelisation)

3. To become the best version of oneself (Integral Development)

4. To be mystics having a deep interior life (Mystical Union).

Each stage moves the person along the continuum, from childhood, adolescence, then young adulthood to adult in the faith. This momentum is the stuff of good preaching and pastoral care. The two must go together. The priest and the congregation need to understand the stages of spiritual development and commit to a journey of growth towards the highest level possible. We are all sinners on pilgrimage to full union with Christ.

Vocation

When people hear vocation, they hear priest, religious, etc. But vocation is much more fundamental to the disciple's life. We all have a vocation! Because God had made us unique, he has called us in unique ways. Each of us has a purpose to fulfil (vocation) that only the individual can full. This life-purpose is prior to the second level of vocation; how we live it out – single, married, religious, lay consecrated or in priestly ministry. Herb Alphonso SJ, in his wonderful little book *Discovering your Personal Vocation: The search for meaning through the Spiritual Exercises*, lays out a pathway to discovering your personal vocation.

Alphonso, a Jesuit, roots his method in the Ignatian notion of election. Each soul is called specially by God for a sacred task. To discover your personal vocation is to discover your personal relationship with Jesus Christ. Only this deep interior sense of call and election would anchor the person in his or her journey of discipleship. Because of this primary vocation, people discover and live their secondary vocation with great depth and dedication. The problem for priest and congregation is that we try to live the outer vocation – single, married, religious, lay consecrated and priesthood – without a deep sense of the primary vocation.

If the priest and his whole congregation know and are living out of the primary vocation, then they are well on the way to sanctity and mission. When we spend time trying to get people to do things for the Church, before assisting them to know how they are before God we end up with *ministries* but not the manifestation of the Kingdom that Jesus expects from the Church.

Missionary Discipleship

When we know God's call and are living our personal vocation, energy is unleashed. We begin to align with God's plan in our world and in our life. The focus becomes then *to bend my heart to God's will* in things big and small. This is aligning my life with God's call.

Here, at the second stage, we are compelled to share this overwhelming grace with others. This is the heart of the missionary discipleship. Having encountered Christ through personal vocation, we witness to Christ in everything we do. Because Christ has captivated our hearts and imagination, and we are consciously bending our hearts and will to Christ, we pick up on the subtle opportunities for witnessing to Christ. Many times I have sat next to someone on an aeroplane and had a conversation the person was dying to have. Several times I have asked, at the end of conversation, if he or she wanted absolution. If we are attentive to Christ many opportunities arise to share Christ with others. This is what it means to be a missionary disciple. This is where Pope Francis wants to lead all Catholics today.

Integral Development

In our early stages of spiritual development, we are often hold binary propositions. In Fowler's stages of spiritual development his second stage is binary. At this stage justice and similar notions come to the fore. When people stay too long at this stage it becomes fundamentalism. There is no joy, no nuance, no subtlety. The world is black or white. Catholic fundamentalism is on the rise in the West. It is condemnatory, it proposes simplistic propositions, its weapon of choice is a *dubia*.

Integral development, on the other hand, is both a way of seeing the world and a stage of spiritual development. As a way of seeing the world, we see people in the various stages of human growth and know they have the capacity to move from one stage to another, to a more human stage of development. This is a much more textured and complex world where God is always inviting the person to discover and live their vocation. Here, there is always room for growth and Christ is the initiator of this growth. This is Fowler's stage 4 and 5.

The deep conflicts in the Church today, brought about by those who are openly and aggressively opposing the Holy Father, can be understood here. They are stuck in a binary stage of spiritual development and Pope Francis is in a much more advanced stage, where paradox and the capacity to grow are part and parcel of his way of seeing the world. Chapter Eight of *Amores Laetitia* is invested with paradoxical language and images. Catholic fundamentalists want a simple yes or no. This was also at the heart of the conflict between Jesus and the religious leaders of his day. Nothing has changed.

Mystical Union

The image of abiding in Christ is central to St John's Gospel. Jesus says, "I am the vine and you are the branches", and further, "Make your home in me as I make mine in you" (Jn 15:1,4). This knowledge, existential ground that we are in Christ as Christ is in us, is the pinnacle of the spiritual life, Fowler's highest stage of spiritual development. Additionally, Jesus promises if we love him the Father, Son and Spirit will come and make their home in us (Jn 14:23).

In this stage the soul knows union with God. There is energy welling up and a deep sense of belonging to God. The soul moves from contrition (the early stage) to gratitude (the middle stage) to compassion (the ultimate stage). These dispositions of the heart are the best way to understand where you are in the spiritual journey. As the soul falls deeper in love with Christ and is immersed more and more in the Trinitarian love, compassion springs forth for all the world to see. You cannot fake this. To this, Pope Francis also witnesses.

St Theresa of Avila proposes a great image of prayer as watering a garden. The first stage is the well. We do the work pulling the water up every day. The second stage is the aqueduct. There is still work, but the water is now flowing a little more. The third stage is the stream, where there is a constant flow of water and the work is very light. The fourth stage is the rain: God waters the garden and serves the soul as it enters into mystical union.

Conclusion

Whether you follow Fowler's stages of development, or St Theresa of Avila's, stages of prayer, the tradition speaks of spiritual development. This is vital both for preacher and for congregation. A major challenge arises when a minister is stuck at an earlier stage of development and imposes a static model of Catholicism on people, as if it is the only view of Catholicism. This stunts the people and robs them of the joy of the Gospel. It also robs them of the possibility of spiritual growth. It is vital that the preacher has a sense of the dynamism of the spiritual life, and that this is conveyed continually to the People of God.

In this chapter I focused on the disposition of the preacher. I believe the listeners always hear that disposition, conveyed through the homily. I also believe this is the greatest gift the preacher can give to the congregation. This stretch, this grace, this action in the soul of the preacher is an unconscious, hidden communication to the listener. This is why a good homily takes time. Time for us to grow; time for God to do his work in and through us. Homily preparation is not like microwave cooking; it is slow cooking in a crockpot.

Says St Paul:

I planted the seed, Apollos watered it, but God has been making it grow. So neither the one who plants nor the one who waters is anything, but only God, who makes things grow. The one who plants and the one who waters have one purpose, and they will each be rewarded according to their own labour. For we are co-workers in God's service; you are God's field, God's building (1 Cor 3: 6-9).

We cannot move from stage to stage except through God's grace. Nor will we move if we do not believe, do everything we can to dispose ourselves to God and trust the God who caused us to grow.

CHAPTER 11

FEEDBACK

"Feedback is the breakfast of champions". This may seem like a cliché at first glance. But it contains a deep truth. To improve continuously as a preacher, you need ongoing and structured feedback. Continuous improvement requires a strategy.

Over the years I have elicited feedback in several ways. After doing a preaching course with "Preaching Rocket", I adopted their method of a weekly homily review. I selected five people who would regularly be in the congregation to do this review. They were selected because I believed them to be thoughtful and honest and would not tell me what I wanted to hear. They were independent thinkers. But most importantly, they loved the Church and their priests and would not give criticism for the sake of criticism. They were committed to continuous improvement.

Over time the feedback allowed me to see how the message was being received by my congregation. Sometimes I thought I communicated the main idea of the homily, however the evaluators all had very different perspectives on it. There were times I thought I communicated an action step for the congregation: the feedback showed that it was either unclear or not communicated at all. Sometimes I thought the homily was a dismal failure, only to realise it struck a chord with some on the review team.

Homily evaluation pays great dividends. For me, the greatest benefit is an objective measure which I have been able to internalise. I am a much better critic of the homily now than before I began the evaluation process. It takes courage, but it is worth it. Many will object and tell you it is disrespectful to evaluate the priest. Tell them you are committed to grow and you need their honest loving assistance.

Through the process of evaluation I have discovered unconscious habits that annoy my congregation. But I also discovered the strengths I needed to build upon. Sometimes I hit the mark; other times I did not. It was always interesting to see people's different perspectives and what they got from the homily. Through continuous feedback you will grow in the art and skill of preaching. If you take one action away from this book, commit to soliciting feedback as often as possible. Bring together a team of reviewers in every congregation to whom you preach regularly. Tell them you need their help. Produce the homily evaluation form in an editable format and ask them to fill it out and email it back to you every week (See Homily Rating Form, page 122).

If you want to go a step further, give them a copy of this book so they think more deeply about the goal and expectation of preaching. Then spend time prayerfully reviewing the feedback you receive.

If you are the senior pastor in your parish or live in a cluster, or work with other priests and deacons, introduce the idea of evaluation and host a weekly meeting to review each other's homilies and the feedback each received from their five people. This simple discipline will yield great fruit and will move your parish ministry to a very different level.

The great dissatisfaction I hear about most often is the lack of discipline or standards around preaching. If we took this criticism seriously and worked diligently, with small steps, to improve our preaching, it will be a great gift to Christ and his people.

CONCLUSION

I hope this little book on Christian preaching has helped you on your journey. My intention is simple, to open a way for the preacher of today to see his vocation to preaching as a sacred call. This call (vocation) needs to be responded to with depth and compassion. It is my hope these pages would have encouraged you to go to the depth of our Christian tradition and explore the word anew. I hope that what shone through these pages more than anything else is the invitation of Christ to your soul.

I pray that through these pages a birthing takes place, as Christ invites you to a new and deeper relationship with him. It is only through this relationship that the preacher will have the words and the power to invite today's listeners to "see with their eyes, hear with their ears, understand with their hearts and turn", for the Lord to heal them (Mt 13:15).

We live in a culture where the word of God is often heard. People believe they have heard the biblical story before it is read by the preacher. They believe it is a good story given by a good teacher. Because the word has been so available, and yet so inaccessible through credible witnesses, there is a dullness to the reception of the word in the late Western modern person. This dullness is the prevailing culture that is now hostile to the Word. What worked for the preacher five or ten years ago, will not work for the contemporary preacher.

Paul VI has famously said: "Modern [woman or] man listens more willingly to witnesses than to teachers, and if [she or] he does listen to teachers, it is because they are witnesses" (*Evangelii Nuntiandi* 41). Today the bar has been raised even more. To be heard amidst all the many words and digital communications that are on offer today, modern preachers need to live the full depth of the message of Christ. They need to be mystics knowing mystical union with Christ who is the vine.

It is the smell of holiness, the intimate connection with Christ, the depth of soul and the capacity to initiate others into the sacred mysteries that our people are looking for. Even a whiff, a glimpse or a flicker will awake the sleeping soul and invite it to rebirth. As priests, ministers and pastors we spend so much time on so many things. At the end of the day, Jesus's word to St Martha is as relevant to us as it was to her, "but few things are needed – or indeed only one. Mary has chosen what is better, and it will not be taken away from her" (Lk 10:42).

For the sake of your ministry, for the sake of your people, for the sake of Christ, choose the one thing that is necessary: sit at the feet of Christ as a disciple listening to his every word. Then you will have a word to speak to this generation, a word of hope, a word of love and a word of life.

St John Chrysostom reflecting on the challenge of preaching said:

For the public are accustomed to listen not for profit but for pleasure, sitting like critics of tragedies, and of musical entertainments, and that facility of speech against which I declaimed just now, in this case becomes desirable, even more than in the case of barristers, where they are obliged to contend against one another. A preacher then should have loftiness of mind, that he may correct this disorderly and unprofitable pleasure on the part of the multitude, and be able to lead them over to a more useful way of hearing, that his people may follow and yield to him, and that he may not be led away by their own humours, and this is not possible to arrive at, except by two means: indifference to their praise, and the power of preaching well. (*Treatise Concerning the Priesthood*)

Let us pray, you and I, that we will be better and better preachers every day. This will not happen unless we are willing to fall into the hands of the living God.

Homily Rating Form

Preacher's Name: _____   Date: _____

Church: _____

Location: _____

Liturgy of the Day: _____

Your Age: [ ] 18 – 39   [ ] 40 – 59   [ ] 60 +

Please rate the homily from 1 to 5 according to each of the criteria below. 1 is **Very Weak** and 5 is **Excellent**. If a feature does not apply at all, circle NA (Not Applicable), but only when really required.

SPIRITUAL VALUE						
Did the homily speak to your heart?	1	2	3	4	5	NA
Did it move you to examine your life?	1	2	3	4	5	NA
Was it relevant to your daily life?	1	2	3	4	5	NA
Did it prompt you to take action?	1	2	3	4	5	NA
Name the action						

CONTENT						
Was the homily rooted in Scripture of the day?	1	2	3	4	5	NA
Was it Christ-centred?	1	2	3	4	5	NA
Did the homily explain the Church's teaching?	1	2	3	4	5	NA
Did it express the central theme clearly?	1	2	3	4	5	NA
Were the illustrations and stories helpful?	1	2	3	4	5	NA
Was the homily focused on a main idea?	1	2	3	4	5	NA
Name the big idea						

STRUCTURE						
Did the homilist engage you from the start?	1	2	3	4	5	NA
Did ideas flow smoothly and clearly?	1	2	3	4	5	NA
Did the homilist end effectively?	1	2	3	4	5	NA

DELIVERY						
Did the homilist hold your attention throughout?	1	2	3	4	5	NA
Was the homilist personal, authentic, sincere?	1	2	3	4	5	NA
Did the homilist show familiarity with the material?	1	2	3	4	5	NA
Did you hear the homilist clearly and distinctly?	1	2	3	4	5	NA
Was the homilist's posture good and gestures appropriate?	1	2	3	4	5	NA
Did the homilist have a pleasant and inviting demeanour?	1	2	3	4	5	NA

LENGTH OF HOMILY   [ ] Too Short   [ ] Too Long   [ ] About Right

Overall Rating: MESSAGE	1	2	3	4	5
Overall Rating: DELIVERY	1	2	3	4	5

GENERAL COMMENTS:

Selected Bibliography

De Lubac, Henri. *Church, Paradox & Mystery*. 3 July 2019, www.crossroadsinitiative.com/media/articles/the-church-paradox-and-mystery-henri-de-lubac/

Francis. *Joy of the Gospel* (*Evangelii Gaudium*). USCCB, 2013

Francis. *Lumen Fidei*. 29 June 2013, www.vatican.va/content/francesco/en/encyclicals/documents/papa-francesco_20130629_enciclica-lumen-fidei.html

Lamming, George. *Coming Home: Conversations II: Western Education and the Caribbean Intellectual*. St Martin: House of Nesesi Publishers,1995.

Liturgy Office of the Bishop's Conference, England and Wales. "General Instruction of the Roman Missal", 2011, www.liturgyoffice.org.uk/Resources/GIRM/Documents/GIRM.pdfLectionary

Lynch, William. *Christ and Apollo: The Dimensions of the Literary Imagination*. Sheed & Ward, 1960.

Paul VI. *Mysterium Fidei*. 3 September 1965, www.vatican.va/content/paul-vi/en/encyclicals/documents/hf_p-vi_enc_03091965_mysterium.html

Ratzinger, Joseph. *Jesus of Nazareth*. Part Two. Ignatius Press, 2011.

Satterlee, Craig A. *Ambrose of Milan's Method of Mystagogical Preaching*. Liturgical Press, 2002.

"Zander Crauwcamp: Bible Matters." *YouTube,* www.youtube.com/watch?v=wNWvxexMri0

www.ingramcontent.com/pod-product-compliance
Lightning Source LLC
Chambersburg PA
CBHW060944040426
42445CB00011B/989